Stone Age Alpha

by

Edward Peterson

P.C.D. Ruthven Books

P.C.D. Ruthven Books
PH3 1JD

The front cover designed by the author is illustrating megalithic symbolic designs of the lozenge and oval shapes symbolising the eyes, nose and mouth of the sacred seal.

The inset photographs on front cover are as follows :

Spiral symbols from Achnabreck, Argyll.
Silbury Hill, Wessex.
Standing Stone at Kirksanton, South Cumbria.
Stonehenge, Wessex.
The back cover is a painting of Queen Nefertiti, by the author, Edward Peterson.

Printed and bound in Malta by Interprint Limited

Foreword

'Alpha', the 'Beginning', has been carefully selected in the title of this book for a number of very important reasons. Alpha is universally accepted as the first letter used in the Greek alphabet, yet the symbol of alpha had been known and used by the Mesolithic people of Britain, Ireland, and Western Europe, long before the Phoenicians portrayed it as a major hieroglyphic symbol.

Academics, writing about the megalithic builders, candidly confirm they are unable to put forward a reason for people having built portal tombs, passage tombs, and henges in the form and manner they did. Scholars have clearly stated that the building of these megalithic edifices remains one of the greatest enigmas of archaeology. This innovative and thought-provoking book gives a comprehensible account as to why these megalithic burial edifices were architecturally designed, sculptured and built, relating directly to the hitherto unknown religious beliefs held by these early humans for many, many thousands of years.

People admire the very fine workmanship of the jewellery manufactured by our ancient craftsmen, and marvel at their skill in producing such intricate designs. Yet until now, no one, as far as the writer is aware, has been able to relate these designs to the ancient sculptured stone culture of the megalithic civilisation prevailing in Britain, Ireland and Western Europe, established long, long before the arrival of the pagan Roman Legions.

One eminent scholar in archaeology has stated clearly as recently as 1995, **'Archaeologists have taken little interest in British rock art because the motifs are entirely abstract. They lack the vivid imagery found in southern Europe, or Scandinavia, where there are numerous drawings of people and animals.'**

As a rock art enthusiast having a reasonable appreciation of this subject whilst researching for years on the fringe of archaeology, I respectfully request that those who are knowledgeable and interested in our pre-history consider this publication as a further tool to assist them to a better understanding. The curtain of obscurity around abstract rock art, and megalithic chambers, has now been lifted, as readers will find as they progress with open minds through this publication.

Introduction

Many people today are more knowledgeable about the heritage and cultures found in other lands, while appearing unaware of our own rich culture. Our heritage is our birthright, unfortunately suppressed and distorted since early times by the pagan Romans, who introduced Latin and Greek with their myths and legends, to the detriment of our own culture and civilisation. The early pious Christian clerics in Britain and Ireland built our Christian Faith from a very early period, based upon the customs and rituals of our struggling indigenous forebears.

Archaeologists are becoming more aware of the value of rock art, and the necessity to study symbols appearing on boulders and on megalithic structures, in order to understand the culture of early people. Some authors, relating to the varied range of our megalithic burial sites, consider that it was the arrival of newcomers from other countries that created the change in design to these early structures, such as portal tombs to long barrows, to round barrows, or to stone circles and henges, and so on. This is not the case, as the religious practices of the indigenous people can be traced from a very early period, proving that there had been a continuity in their religious beliefs, that went hand in hand with their economy. These religious convictions can be traced into our own times.

The rise in popularity of archaeology is witnessed by the increasing number of programmes appearing on television. These highlight how archaeologists require to work closely with other specialists in order to establish the true facts. Early people of southern Britain created many gigantic works of art on the landscape, such as the White Horse of the Cotswolds, and the Cerne Giant near Abbas, Dorset. This form of art can be found on the landscapes of northern Britain carved on boulder rock or as standing stones shaped in the outline of a seal's head and body.

The author, travelling extensively over Britain and Ireland, has established a fresh new insight to and conception of these monuments. The knowledge gained of rock art has led to the discovery of several fascinating megalithic complexes. The colour photographs of one of these sculptured megalithic sites have been examined by the RCAHMS, who confirmed verbally that 'it is quite a unique find for Scotland', and may well be unique to England and Wales. Also discussed in this book is a possible new form of ancient corbelled stone mosaic art, located in a well-known chambered tomb in England dating back to at least c.3000 BC.

Rock art has been known for a considerable time, especially in the Lake District where its potential is only now being fully appreciated by archaeologists and others. This has led to a fresh new approach by Universities to evaluate rock art more precisely to create a better understanding of archaeology and history. Readers, after studying this book, will more easily relate to our pre-history, in turn assisting them to recognise many as yet unidentified chambers and tombs.

Contents

List of photographs and sketches

Fig. No.	Description	Origin	Page No.

List of colour photographs

CHAPTER 1

Floods Follow Deglaciation

In 1650, James Usher, the learned Irish Archbishop of Armagh and Primate of All-Ireland, had convinced people that the world had been created at noon on October 23, 4004BC! His remarkable theory came from tracing the genealogy back to Adam in a conscientious study of Egyptian, Greek and Christian texts. It was hailed as an intellectual feat by scholars of that period and his calculation of the earth's age was then printed in the King James authorised version of the Bible.

As the 19th century advanced, many scientists attempted to quantify the Earth's age and today scientists consider that the Earth had begun around 4550 million years ago. Darwin had been one of the scientists who had unsuccessfully made an attempt to place a date on the earth's age. He, however, introduced his theory of evolution, where he theorised that humans had developed from apes, and that we as humans, during our progress, descended as hairy people from the branches of trees, and walked about in a crouched position, similar to the slouching gait of an ape. This theory may no longer be valid if DNA tests on apes reveal no direct link with the genes of humans.

Recent discoveries have found fossilised bacteria in the form of a type of worm whose vertebrae can be linked in origin to salmon. Research in this country is attempting to prove that the vertebrae of man indicate that he had walked in an upright position 4 million years ago. One skeleton called Lucy, found in Hadar, Ethiopia, was of a female, 3 feet tall, dating back 3 million years. The thighs and hips of Lucy indicated that she had walked upright.

During this unimaginable period of time, people developed skills as hunters and stalkers in a world fraught with danger from wild beasts, and extreme changes in climatic conditions, such as earthquakes, volcanic eruptions, and long periods of glaciation and deglaciation. These Ice Age peri-

ods lowered and raised the sea levels, and in turn created gargantuan floods as the ice gradually melted, and the glaciers slowly receded northwards towards the polar regions. The people were aware of these environmental changes, and had adopted a way of life to suit the harshness of the extreme conditions in which they found themselves.

The geological development of Britain, and Ireland, can be witnessed in the changes that had taken place in the mountains of Northern Britain, which at one time had been much higher and were older than the Alps. In Scotland outcrops of Lewisian Gneiss, at 2900 million years old, are among the oldest known rocks throughout the World. These graceful mountains of Northern Britain had at one time maintained ice sheets which were several miles thick, and were decapped through time by successive glaciation and declaciation periods.

One major climatic event that assisted in changing the coastline of Britain and Ireland was the flooding of the continental margin of Europe, possibly around 10 million years ago, creating the Minch and the Hebridean Islands, off the west coast of Northern Britain. Another change to our landscape occurred through the last three main Ice Ages over 600,000 years ago, when the ice not only gouged out our coastal terrain but also sculptured the hills and mountains to form the islands of Britain and Ireland.

Each of these Ice Ages reached a maximum of advance fairly rapidly, to be followed by a more extended period of retreat, giving periods of interglacial climate similar to our own environment of today. At the height of the Devensian Ice Age, from 25,000 to 12,000BC, Britain had in the main been uninhabited, due to average temperatures of - 8°C. Between 11,000 and 10,000BC, ice sheets readvanced over the northern part of Britain, but by 8000BC, a great deal of the country had by then been covered by green forest rather than ice.

The Neanderthal People, who lived 30,000–300,000 years ago, had already established the art of drilling holes, and appear to have had both compassion and spirituality. This can be observed in the compassionate burial of their dead. The Neanderthal graves located at Shanidar in Northern Iraq are a testament to this, and to their humanity. During the caring preparation for the burial of the deceased, they laid a person to rest in a kneeling or foetal position, and on many an occasion would cover the body in red ochre.

This was a formality of returning the dead to the tomb (womb) of mother earth, indicating their belief in life after death. It is apparent that both the Neanderthals and Cro-Magnons had an in-depth knowledge of quarrying and mining in order to obtain sufficient quantities of red ochre for various ceremonies. Evidence of large scale mining and quarrying can be traced to Southern Africa, going back some 100,000 years. The ritual habits of Neanderthal man have a striking similarity with the funerary customs of Mesolithic and Neolithic tomb-builders of Western Europe and the Eastern Mediterranean countries.

The Neanderthals also carried out religious ceremonies to the moon and the stars in the empyrean, as did the Minoans of Crete, who used red ochre as a chosen religious colour on their pillars, and as a background colour in their temples. It is intriguing that many Christian clerics today can trace the wearing of scarlet caps and robes to the symbolism of red ochre. The American Red Indian owes his name to the fact that he covered his body in red ochre during various ritual ceremonies. Aborigines in Australia had also used red dyes in their tribal ceremonies. John Mercer established in recent excavations on the Hebridean Island of Jura that red ochre had been used by the people there during the sixth millennium BC.

The existence of large numbers of Neanderthal people around 300,000 years ago can be traced throughout the whole of Europe, Western Asia and Africa, right up to recent historical times. Their presence, however, cannot be traced to North and South America, Australia, or even to the islands within the Pacific basin. The ancient Greeks referred to attacks on their towns by 'wild men', and then portrayed these most ancient of men on the design of some of their pottery.

Around 40,000 years ago, a new race of people from North Africa and Asia arrived in Europe, some of their origins being traced back in time to Africa 100,000 years ago. They may have confronted the Neanderthals face to face in Germany. As recently as July, 1997, it was announced that DNA samples had been removed from the bones of an ancient Neanderthal in Germany, revealing that the gene structure is completely different from that of Cro-Magnon man. This confirms that we have no genealogical link with Neanderthals, who were obviously a species in their own right. The Cro-Magnon people, known as *Homo sapiens sapiens*, are obviously directly related to present day humans.

Even although the Neanderthal people lived longer than Cro-Magnon man, it appears that around 25,000 years ago, the decline of the Neanderthals accelerated and they became extinct. This may partly be attributed to new strains of viruses and bacteria, introduced unknowingly

by Cro-Magnon people coming into contact with another species. The decline of Neanderthals may also be linked to the reappearance and eventual departure of the last Ice Age, which would have created the problem of flooding and further competition for dwindling supplies of food. The Neanderthal people lived on the lower plains whereas Cro-Magnons selected and dwelt on higher terrain, where they may have escaped the worst of the flooding. This would have inevitably been to the detriment of the Neanderthal race leading to their demise.

The Cro-Magnon hunters travelled from Africa to the Eastern Mediterranean, integrating with others from Asia, and eventually the Danube and the Rhine areas. Then slowly they began to colonise Greece, Italy and Iberia, as they moved westwards following the retreating glaciers to reach and possibly re-populate the coastal belt of Western Europe.

With the arrival of warmer weather, the early inhabitants of our coastline witnessed the gradual melt-down of the many layers of coalesced ice-sheets, that had covered the Grampian Mountains of Northern Britain to a depth of over one mile, whereas Southern England had been a frozen arctic tundra. Due to the changes in sea level a land corridor may at this time have joined the Island of Islay, on the West Coast of Scotland, to Ireland. The sea level in c.10,000BC, in this area, was around 105 feet below what it is today. Both the Irish Sea and the North Sea may have been large tracts of land interspersed by rivers, allowing people and animals to cross at will.

Mesolithic people were among our earliest known industrialists, geologists and miners in Northern Britain. Those who had set up camp in c.8500BC on the Island of Rhum, to manufacture 'microliths', may have witnessed the emergence of the tops of the Grampian mountains through the ice-caps. Here to them was a new land of Alba, emerging through the glacial mantle, a land awakening from its cryogenic slumber, where its rugged, weathered coastline merged with the distant, majestic, mountains that were to give birth to the fast-flowing, sparkling, crystal-clear rivers.

The tranquillity of the mountains and rivers was to change dramatically as each successive layer of ice receded northwards. The oceans rose to unperceived levels with the torrents of water that inundated the coastal plains and land bridges, producing many new rivers which poured torrents of raging melt-water relentlessly forward creating widespread flooding. As the thaw continued, it released the weight and pressure of the ice bearing down on the land, causing the land mass of Northern Britain to rise slowly, compensating for the loss of the ice sheets. Descendants of the coastal dwellers may have witnessed these events, while at the same time a great many would have perished in the turbulent floods that swept through the coastal plains of Britain and Ireland.

In the Great Glen, c.7500BC, the glacial outpouring of water caused the waters of Loch Ness to rise 40 feet higher than they are today. Some glaciers formed a barrier wall linking one mountainside to another creating a natural dam. These glacial dams held back trillions of gallons of water, until their walls finally succumbed and shattered due to the rising temperature and pressure. As these ice dams collapsed, they created gigantic outflows of enormous walls of raging torrents of ice-cold glacial water, that poured mercilessly through Scotland's natural divide of the Great Glen.

These released pent-up waters rose to heights towering over 333 feet at the narrowest gaps between the rugged mountains, disgorging the land before it. Rich glacial mineral deposits were carried unrelentingly forward with these spectacular floods spreading a fertile glacial sediment over the land, and carrying debris eastwards for 60 miles, towards Inverness, and on into the estuary of the Moray Firth.

Floods also moved westwards, pouring into and assisting in the development of Loch Linnhe, a naturally-formed drainage basin for the mountains around Ben Nevis. These colossal, cascading flood-waters rushed forward and met further raging torrents of glacial water which had swept over and around our coastline causing islands to form, such as some of those in the Hebrides, and the islands of Lismore, Gigha and the Isle of Man.

It had been the glacial scouring of the land, with the combined deepening of the sea-channels by a glacier extending down the Firth of Lorne, that changed what had been a peninsula running parallel to Kintyre, transforming it into the islands off the south-west coast of Scotland. Such was the deluge of water, sweeping over and engulfing the country during these deglaciation periods, that the impact of these catastrophic floods was to be felt throughout England, Wales, and Ireland. They added to the glacial melt-down occurring in the Lake District and the Pennines, in Snowdonia, and the mountains of Mourne.

These cataclysms had occurred on more than one occasion and may be one reason for archaeologists having so far been unable to find traces of artefacts relating to the presence of Palaeolithic man in Northern England and in Scotland. Not only had the Mesolithic people of these islands to contend with the deliquescence of the ice sheets in Britain, they also had

to cope with the floods caused by the receding glaciers of Northern Europe.

They were fortunate in one respect, as the low-lying land basin located between the east coast of Britain and Europe was at a much lower level and acted as a reservoir, which at first contained the ever-rising seas, and in turn created an island known today as the Dogger Bank. This island later became a victim to the intensifying seas and eventually became one of the richest fishing-grounds of the North Sea. As the seas continued to build up they cut the land corridor between France and England, forming yet again the English Channel. By this time the land-link between Scotland and Ireland had been severed by the rising tidal flow of the Irish Sea.

Today scientists are warning us of global warming caused by the thinning of the ozone layer in our Northern Hemisphere. However, they are more concerned about the established gap that has appeared in the ozone layer in the Southern Hemisphere. This is presently having a direct effect on the glacial ice continent of Antarctica. This slumbering continent with its coalesced ice shelves is melting at an even greater pace than ever experienced before, due to only a few degrees rise in temperature. This melt-down, as it continues, will raise sea levels and engulf many of the islands of the Pacific, and is likely to create havoc with the coastlines of all the low-lying countries throughout the world.

CHAPTER 2

Life after Deglaciation

After the onslaught of the glacial embrace that covered the Northern Hemisphere, trapping and drowning many varying groups of nomadic humans in areas bordering the icy wastelands, the survivors developed their own separate societies in Western and Eastern Europe, Asia, and America. Many of these scattered groups can be traced back to the ancient civilisations of Africa, the Middle East, and to the Indian Continent.

It has been generally thought that the indigenous people of Western Europe may not have survived the arctic conditions prevailing at the time of our last glacial age. However this may not be the case, considering the independent life-style of the present day nomadic Eskimo, and the Laplander, with their herds of reindeer and Arctic musk-ox. These people today, just as their ancient ancestors had done before them, live and work in a similar type of arctic environment. The ancients who lived around our glacial coastal shores lived like the Eskimo, hunting and stalking animals such as the bear, the elk, the reindeer, and the wolf. A seafaring breakaway group from the inland Lapp people may have landed in Greenland, where their skills in building kayaks could have enabled them to journey on to land in America. One such group that did apparently live most of their lives at sea is the Sjo-same tribe. It has been said that this tribe had a base in the Hebridean Islands of Scotland. Many writers have told stories of seal- and fin-folks living in Northern Britain.

In the 17th and 18th centuries kayaks were discovered near Aberdeen, two of which are held in the anthropological museum at the city's Marischal College, where experts believe them to have been built by the Eskimo people of Greenland. A report in the 18th century by Francis Douglas in his *General Description of the East Coast of Scotland, 1782* describes

'a canoe taken at sea with an Indian man in it about the beginning of this century. He was brought alive to Aberdeen, but died soon after his arrival and could give no account for himself.'

In 1688, the Rev. J.Wallace, of Kirkwall, Orkney, wrote about 'Finmen' seen sailing in canoes around the islands and local people flocking to see them. These sightings may have given confirmation to the beliefs of the existence of fin- or seal-people. Finmen wore tightly fitting skins of seal or walrus, and a special belt to secure themselves into their kayak making themselves and their craft watertight. When seated in their skin-covered kayaks, it appeared from the shore that only their bodies protruded above the surface of the waves. These people may have been related to our early ancient coastal dwellers who paid homage to the seal and were known as the Selkies or Seal People.

Our ancient coastal dwellers were noted as fishermen and sea-farers, who may well have been capable of surviving the sea-crossing to Greenland and to North America. Animals and molluscs found around our shores provided the necessities of life, such as food, clothing and oil for lamps. Tribes, akin to those of the Eagle tribe from Orkney, may have been trapped by the receding ice-caps melting on our northern shores, separating them from their fellow humans in Norway, Iceland and in America. These inhabitants of Orkney and Shetland can trace the stories of the Selkies back to an early period, and believe their ancestors arrived in these islands from Northern Europe long, long before 9000BC, whereas people are known to have reoccupied Southern England before 11,000BC.

Today one cannot imagine the sheer horror of the ferocity of the floods, which the Mesolithic (Mid-Stone Age) people had to endure at this period. Many of these early humans were cave-dwellers living close to the coastal shores, which were at least 100 feet lower than they are to-day. They as nomadic hunters faced drowning in these huge floods. Both our present day fishermen and oil-field operators in the North Sea are continually retrieving flint tools from the sea-bed, confirming the existence of early settlements in the North Sea basin, prior to it being submerged. Many of these flint tools came from Northern Europe, but have also been used by the early inhabitants of the Orkney and Shetland Islands.

As weather conditions improved, the hunting tactics of the people altered and groups from the Iberian Peninsula began to move out of their caves; some headed along the coastline to reintegrate with the coastal dwellers of North Western Europe; others moved towards North Africa; while some journeyed eastwards along the Mediterranean. This movement of people may well have been a form of two-way traffic, as others from the east were also travelling to the west and to the north.

In c.8500BC on the Hebridean Island of Rhum, off the west coast of

Scotland, voyagers, perhaps from Northern Europe, set up a camp while searching for suitable rock to manufacture microliths. These early people may have supplied microliths to established, industrial units manufacturing flint tool implements, possibly in Southern England. In Ireland the oldest, known settlement, dating back to 7500 BC, can be found at Mount Sandel on the River Bann, south of Coleraine. Present evidence points to Mesolithic people having commenced to inhabit the west coast of Ireland c.9000BC. By around 8000BC Europe was mainly free of ice, while the actual end of the Ice Age has been placed at c.4000BC.

Mesolithic people obtained their hunting skills by carefully observing and studying animals and birds, and their predators. This basic understanding of nature was essential to them, as their own survival depended on this fundamental knowledge. They were aware of the aggressive, territorial behaviour of all creatures towards one another. The coastal dwellers were specially aware of how fish would swallow fish; the seal would then eat the fish, falling prey to Orca, the killer whale. Shoals of herring came under attack from pods of killer whales, which would stun the silver darlings by creating a thunderous crack with a sweep of their massive tails. Many stunned fish floated to the surface to be devoured by scavenging gulls and sea-eagles.

Man, as a predator himself, was mindful of how, in the process of obtaining food, birds and other rapacious creatures would squabble with one another, as they snapped up and devoured their quarry. These were the basic facts that these early people were taught from birth. They were trained how to hunt and overcome their prey, and to consume an enemy by overwhelming or by simply gobbling him up. This was a daily occurrence, in an environment where only the fittest and strongest could survive.

The intertwined artwork of early people in Northern Britain and Ireland was later illustrated by zoomorphic creatures biting and swallowing one another. This indicates how they had carefully studied life, and how they lived and interacted with nature and with one another. From the earliest days they had established that with resolution and determination they could overcome their adversaries in a similar manner.

As animals were important to the survival of the ancient people in Europe and Asia, they were concerned about the steady decline of the wild animal herds, which at one time roamed freely throughout Europe and the Middle East. This was a problem created by man himself, as he had been hunting all forms of animals almost into extinction. (We face a simi-

lar problem today, with the decline of fish stocks in the seas around the world.) In the marshlands of Denmark, a large dugout canoe had been found dating back to c.7000BC, along with evidence indicating that off-shore fishermen used nets to catch deep-sea fish.

The oldest and most intact human remains ever found in North America are the skull and bones of Kennewick Man, said to be a Caucasian dating back to 7300BC. This may indicate that some early Americans were of Indo-European stock, and may have migrated from Northern Europe over a land bridge exposed in the Bering Sea 12,000 years ago. The skull is said to have similar features to those of Patrick Stewart, the 20th century actor and *Star Trek* hero!

It is highly probable that during the last Ice Age people lived on the Island of St.Kilda surrounded by ice-floes. At that time this island had been much larger with wide varieties of trees, although today it is treeless. The gently sloping ground leading to the sea has now been eroded by the relentless pounding of the Atlantic waves, leaving massive daunting cliffs making a difficult approach to this island sanctuary of early man. The cliffs were the sanctuary for many sea birds such as the gannet and fulmar. Early man extracted oil from the fulmar to light his lamps, which along with other sea birds provided food, foot-wear, and clothing. Feathers of sea birds were supplied by the people of St. Kilda for bedding used by our troops during the 1914–18 war.

By c.7000BC the land link between Scotland and Ireland had been severed, and around 6000BC Britain had been cut off yet again from Europe, becoming an island of inland waterways and marshes. Hunters witnessed many of their fertile hunting grounds in Yorkshire and Lincolnshire being submerged under water. In the hill forests of the Pennines, animals such as the elk were facing extinction. This created a further awareness in hunters of the need to conserve the wild animals, by domesticating the tamer animals, such as pigs and goats. They had also set about opening up the forests by hacking down trees with stone axes, burning the brush-wood, and clearing stones away to form small glades in the forest. There they rejuvenated the land, and sowed early varieties of wheat called emmer and einkorn, along with a wild type of barley, for the benefit of humans and animals alike. In the Orkney and Shetland Islands another use for the barley and emmer was in the making of a strong brew of liquor.

CHAPTER 3

The Dawn of a New Age

*I*t was over 8000 years ago that the Mesolithic people in our Western European civilisation began to erect stone monuments over their sacred dead, and in so doing paid homage to the whale and the seal. They believed that the whale was the first creature to inhabit the seas, as confirmed in the Holy Scriptures. Humans had from earliest days worshipped the sun, stars and the moon, and, as coastal dwellers, combined the worship of the firmament with the worship of sacred sea-creatures. This was an integral belief that became a part of their way of life, forming the basis of our early western civilisation.

This belief and the strong faith of the Mesolithic coastal dwellers had been handed down to the megalithic tomb-builders. These burial chambers were one of the ceremonial centres and gathering places for each family within a tribal territory. Much later these structures also became the tribal boundary attribute to warn unwanted incomers against making claim to the indigenous people's tribal lands.

The megalithic tomb-builders clearly had an in-depth knowledge of their natural surroundings. They had been well aware of the evolution of plantlife, observing the slow spiral movement of plants and trees creeping ever upwards as if stretching to reach the heavens. Both plants and creatures depended on the sun and rain to provide heat and water as nourishment to stimulate growth. This is one reason for the ancestors of Mesolithic man having added the meaningful spiral of life symbols to boulders and rocks throughout the world.

The stones used to build megalithic monuments are considered by many people to have been roughly quarried stones, then carefully selected and erected by the builders. Yes, they were quarried and painstakingly selected, but then many were sculptured to a precise standard, by using hand-held hard stone to chip, flake and peck, and in some cases grind the stone to a

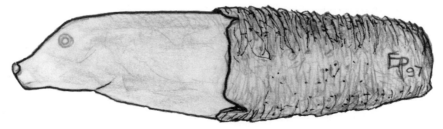

Figure1 *Flint knife from 'Bann Flakes'.*

smooth finish. What should not be forgotten is that early people had already learned how to shape and dress stone to a pre-determined shape, and were more than capable of drilling holes. A good example of a sliver of flint, shaped and dressed to form a knife blade, was found in the River Bann, in Ireland; the blade had been honed and polished in the outline of the sacred seal, as shown in Figure 1.

By 4500BC flint tools and weapons were being manufactured with an individual design and shape, which can be related directly to the sacred seal, such as the simple flint knife wrapped with moss and secured by twine at the handle. The design concept for the common scissors, blacksmith's tongs, pliers, etc. can be traced back through time to the head of a sea-creature, with the eye of the sea-mammal becoming the pivotal point, and the short leg of the implement illustrating the mouth which opens and closes to cut or to hold an object. It is feasible that flints, among them some with the outline of a seal head and some crescent-shaped, were used to barter for goods.

These early people built the megalithic monuments on raised ground to be ever closer to the heavens, where the all-important rays from the sun could penetrate the dark passageways leading to the tombs. Here they believed the rays of the sun came into direct contact with the remains of their departed, generating new life to the deceased.

They were only too aware of the severe climatic changes that occurred; this may be yet another consideration that led the Neolithic people to build their tombs on raised ground, to be free of the fear of flooding. From the vantage points of the hilltops, they were able to survey their land around them, and at a later date to identify intruders such as the incoming farmers with their flocks approaching their water-logged domain. These megalithic structures gave a clear, warning signal to unwelcome incomers, advising them of the tribal ownership of the land through which they were passing.

As coastal dwellers and sea-farers, they were skilled in navigating to and from the lands of the Mediterranean. Every schoolboy realises that it is essential for a good navigator to have a sure knowledge of mathematics to plot his course in conjunction with the position of the moon and the stars in the skies, and to take into account the tidal drift and changing sea currents when setting a course offshore. This mathematical skill was used by the megalithic tomb-builders as they methodically plotted the rise and fall of the sun and the moon, so that rays from these heavenly bodies would illuminate their tombs at precise ceremonial periods of the year. During the winter solstice the sun penetrates the ancient passageways of Maes Howe Chambered Tomb, in Orkney, Scotland, and at Newgrange, Co. Meath, in Ireland. These predetermined settings for the sun's rays of light had been calculated to illuminate the passageway and slowly filter the rays of light to the very the heart of the inner chamber.

The light from the sun was a very important part of early man's belief, which was developing towards a new faith. In the New Testament it is recorded that Christ himself placed much emphasis on light as an integral part of our Christian faith, as in St.John, Chapter 8, Verse 12, Then spake Jesus again unto them, saying,

'I am the light of the world : he that followeth me shall not walk in darkness, but shall have the light of life.'

It is obvious that Christ himself had been very much aware of the significance of light, not only to the people of the Eastern Mediterranean but to the civilisations of men and women throughout Europe. It becomes increasingly clear that early people from both Europe and the Middle East were moving forward together seeking a new way of life. Both cultures from east and west were looking upwards to the firmament for the coming of the Messiah.

In Britain the inhabitants referred to the Messiah as 'Yesu', and much later in *The Canterbury Tales* Geoffrey Chaucer refers to Christ as Jesu. Jesu is also named in all the early sacred manuscripts, such as the lovely haunting melody of *Jesu, Joy of Man's Desiring*, Bach's Cantata 147. The stirring singing of *Jerusalem*, written by William Blake, said to be a confirmed Druid, gives the impression that Jesus did walk in ancient times in these green and pleasant lands, and I am inclined to agree. The name, Jesu, may have been known in Britain as well as in Galilee, where the distinction was made by referring to Christ as Jesus of Nazareth, or Jesus the Nazarene.

To attempt to comprehend the development of these ancient societies

and their movement towards Christianity, it is necessary to examine and confirm the existence of the early 'seal' culture, by re-examining some of the hundreds of megalithic monuments found throughout Britain and Ireland. These early people had made a record of their tribal origins and beliefs, some inscribed on stone, others displayed as artwork, and jewellery, relating in many, many cases to the sculptured design of their sacred seal.

In Britain, and Ireland, there were several groups of people who occupied and controlled these islands. The first were the coastal dwellers and seafarers, who had taken shelter in caves from the icy blasts of the glaciation period that shrouded Western Europe, Southern Britain, Gaul and Iberia. As the climate improved people came out of their cave-dwellings, meeting other groups who may have arrived from the Baltic and Scandinavian countries, and then joined with others from Gaul and the Mediterranean.

As people arrived in Southern England from Gaul and Iberia, they continued to move up the west coast of Britain to the Isle of Man, Wales, the Solway coast, on northwards into the Clyde estuary, and further north to Orkney, and the Shetland Islands. In the established settlements they integrated with others who had travelled south from Orkney, Shetland, and even Northern Europe. Arrivals to the River Clyde found that the River Clyde and the River Forth had at one time divided Scotland in two, forming a tidal sea-channel that joined the west coast to the east coast.

Evidence of this has been found in the upper reaches of the River Forth, where a skeleton of a whale was found with a Neolithic antler axe embedded in its skull. (In March 1997, a 40 ft. whale swam up the River Forth, to die on the land rather than out at sea. The skull of this creature is now housed at Deep Sea World, North Queensferry, on the River Forth.) Further evidence of this sea-channel can be established from records that in 81AD Agricola had camped near Stirling, where his brother-in-law Tacitus had at first thought that Scotland was two nations divided by the marshlands of the Clyde and Forth valley. He records that the firths of **'Clota and Bodotria, being carried far inland by tides from opposite seas, are separated by a narrow stretch of land'**.

This area had been part of the Iapetus Ocean, an ocean covering an ancient forest which had been part of the super-continent of Laurentia over 400 million years ago. It was not until very much later after several glaciation and deglaciation periods that the River Clyde flowed westwards into the Irish Sea. The Roman name for this sea was Hibernicus Oceanus.

(Hibernia is the Latin name for Ireland.) This was the sea governed by the Iberian people, who sailed around the ever enchanting Hebridean Isles. It must be noted that the sea with its western islands was not referred to as 'The Celtic Sea'. At this period the indigenous inhabitants of Britain and Ireland were a race apart and were stated by the Romans to be taller than the Celts of Europe.

The megalithic tomb-builders may well have been looked upon as our Mesolithic colonists, building their ceremonial monuments high on the hilltops, to worship the empyrean and to pay homage to their sea-gods, such as the seal, thus enabling the all-seeing eyes of the seal to have sight of both land and water, as well as being closer to the skies. They had observed how the mammals and fish in the oceans, rivers and lakes would jump clear out of the water, or swim upstream in their endeavour to scale the rapids and waterfalls, believing implicitly that the fish also wanted to reach Utopia.

This is a central belief in Japan, where Japanese parents have a special ceremony for their male children each year when paper cut-outs of carp are suspended from the ceilings of their homes, the heads pointing directly to the skies. The Japanese instruct their sons to grow as strong and determined as the carp as it swims up-river and leaps the waterfalls to be closer to the sun. It is interesting too that the sun is the main emblem of the Japanese flag. This is why the salmon had been singled out by our forebears, as, like the carp, it too swam up our rivers, jumping and clearing the waterfalls to reach the spawning grounds located hundreds of feet above sea-level, to be nearer to the sky.

The early people in Britain and Europe realised that seals and certain species of whales slept in the sea in an upright position, known today as bottling. They believed that these creatures were attempting to pay homage to the heavens above. This is why they had sculptured these stone pillars and erected them in an upright position to represent seals/whales stretching upwards as if reaching for the heavens.

It does emerge, after studying our megalithic structures, that there were at least two main sea-creatures to which the early people of Western Europe paid homage. These sacred sea-mammals were the whale and the seal. The whale is mentioned in the first book of the Old Testament, in the first chapter of Genesis, verse 21, which reads:

'And God created great whales, and every living creature that moveth, which the waters brought forth abundantly, after

their kind, and every winged fowl after his kind; and God saw that it was good.'

The Book of Genesis is not only the first book of The Old Testament, it is also the oldest book known to man. Some say that the Book of Genesis can be traced back to c.3500BC; however the words in this book may have in the first instance been passed down orally from descendants of Cro-Magnon man, along with customs passed down from the Neanderthals to the Cro-Magnons.

It becomes very apparent that early man indubitably considered that whales were the first creatures created by God, and to him this meant Alpha, the 'Beginning' of life on earth. Alpha, as every schoolboy or girl knows, is the first letter in the Greek alphabet, and it is the Greeks who are said to have been the originators of the alphabet. However, let us ponder on the origin of 'Alpha', and its acute angular symbol, which may go back through time to the Stone Age. Mesolithic man built many of his structures and artefacts to include the acute angle within a basic shape or design pattern, as will be observed as this book unfolds. There are indications that, long before the Greeks and the Phoenicians, the peoples of Western Europe had used not only the symbol of 'alpha' but the symbols of 'delta', 'X', and 'omega'.

Mesolithic people throughout the world had obviously discussed the origin of man, with whom they associated the whale and the seal. This strongly-held belief had been adopted and accepted as part of their basic religious faith, which was passed down from the earliest time to the Christian era, as they paid homage to gods and to God in the heavens. Early people were aware of the Book of Genesis, that the whale had been the first creature to enter the seas, and they had deduced that it begat the seal, and the seal, they believed, begat man; they related the seal to 'Alpha' as the Beginning. It becomes clear that at the early transitional stage of accepting Christianity, people in Britain still had their basic pagan understanding of 'Alpha'. At this time they were being persecuted by the Romans, and their faith was under severe strain. This is another reason for God to clarify and emphasise the true meaning of 'alpha' and 'omega', when He spoke these words to John, in the Book of Revelation: **'I am Alpha and Omega, the first and the last.'**

This is mentioned several times in The Revelation of John – Chapter 1, Verse 8; Chapter 21, Verse 6; and Chapter 22, Verse 13 – and gives an idea of the importance God placed on these words and their significance for all mankind. People today may not fully understand the underlying importance of this message, but early people in different parts of the world, including Britain and Ireland, had been gradually developing their belief in the Book of Genesis and were moving towards a new faith, such as Christianity, embodying many of their own beliefs, in which 'Alpha' and 'Omega' had played a major part for many thousands of years. This is one reason why followers of Christ may have had a captive audience who grasped and accepted Christianity wholeheartedly, as they were fully aware of the substance of such a message.

People throughout the world still pay homage to the whale; the coastal Indians of North America refer to the eye of the whale as belonging to the first creature to have seen and witnessed the heavens above. On many of the American Indian carvings of a whale, the eyes are depicted as strikingly prominent, while other tribes have a ceremonial head-dress of a whale. The early Europeans placed more emphasis on the eye and the head of the seal, and in many instances this eye was shown as a spiral, linked with another spiral for the snout of the seal or as a triangle or even a diamond pattern.

Paying homage to sea-creatures was not only a Western European phenomenon, as throughout the world similar beliefs were held by other races, such as the people of Hawaii who consider the shark as one of their ancestral spirits, and the Aborigine people of Western Australia who believe that their ancestral spirits are linked with the dugong, a distant cousin of the seal.

Knowing of my research on this subject, Dr.J.S.Black, from Marlborough, sent the following newspaper cutting dating back to 31-12-93, which gives a guide to the burial customs of the Fijians.

FIJI funeral flotilla escorted by sharks

INSUVA, FIJI

A SCHOOL of sharks appeared suddenly and spectacularly in the harbour this week and accompanied the funeral flotilla of Ratu Sir Penaia Ganilau, the Fijian President, out to sea.

They surfaced during the ceremonial 21-gun salute in front of the government vessel, Tovuto, which carried his coffin to his home island of Taveuni, where he will be entombed tomorrow.

Ratu Ganilau was a direct descendant of Dakuwaqa, the ancestral shark god, and mourners had anticipated that sharks would appear as the flotilla left Suava, the capital.

Women mourners, dressed in black, lined up along the seawall, wept and pro-

claimed that he was truly a great chief, and that his shark escort reaffirmed the bloodline from Dakuwaqa, the Daily Post reported.

Sightings of even a single shark in the harbour are rare.

Ratu Ganilau was Governor-General at the time of the two anti-Indian military coups by Fijians in 1987, and became President when Fiji was declared a republic later that year.

More than 6,000 mourners are expected in his home village of Somosomo for the traditional funeral rites. Hundreds of cattle and pigs will be slaughtered to feed the mourners at the funeral feast; the mourners have also taken traditional gifts of food to the people of Taveuni.

The burial ceremony and feast held on Fiji may well have been similar to the type of farewell to the dead made by our forefathers, who at the same time paid homage to the seal with its large all-seeing eyes and wide mouth.

The eyes and open mouths of sea-creatures such as seals and whales have played a very significant role in the lives of our ancient ancestors, as readers will find as this book unfolds our ancient heritage. Two sets of eyes are shown in the sketch of a face-mask (Fig.2) imaged on bark cloth, from the Gazelle Peninsula, New Britain, 19th–20th century.

Figure 2 *Face mask.*

The American Indians are portraying on this face-mask the eyes and the head of a crocodile, which to them represented an animal spirit, the mask being worn during nocturnal ceremonies by dancers holding snakes. The design of the crocodile mask is interesting, as the two main circles, shown prominently above the head of the crocodile, are in fact eyes looking down as if watching the reptile. These two dominating circles are very similar to the double discs depicted on the Symbol Stones found in Britain and Ireland. The double disc symbol is portraying the eyes of a sea-creature, as well as illustrating a plan view of a double henge or a pair of Round Barrows, to be discussed later in this book.

Hehaka Sapa, North American Oglala Sioux, 1930–31, wrote:-

'The power of the world always works in circles, and everything tries to be round. In the old days...all our power came to us from the sacred hoop of the nation and so long as the hoop was unbroken the people flourished.'

This may have been only part of the thinking process of early man when at Stonehenge he erected Sarsen Stones, capped by a continuous ring of lintels, which to them was also a continuation of the theme of the quoit placed by their ancestors on top of the orthostats to form a portal dolmen.

The quoit had been used as the stone sealing the top of the main chamber at Newgrange, Ireland, and at Maes Howe, Orkney, and can also be found in the roof construction of circular barrows. Later it was added as the capstone covering the wedge-shaped tombs. Even into our own time at burial sites the capstone can still be seen raised either on plinths or laid directly on the ground.

The early religious beliefs of the people of Western Europe can be traced to the island of Madagascar, where groups of standing stones had been erected. This assists in proving that our ancestors were natural sea-farers and explorers who as early colonisers travelled great distances, always retaining their inspired faith.

CHAPTER 4
Megalithic Tomb-Builders

Many of the megalithic burial sites were built many thousands of years before the pyramids of Egypt. These impressive structures can be found in Western Europe, from Sweden to Spain, North Africa, and on through the Mediterranean to Palestine where in the Golan Heights, in the fields east of Gamia, it is possible to find several dolmens, most dating back to 4000BC. Dolmens are found at several other sites around Golan and Galilee. These structures have also been traced to Asia Minor and on towards India.

The oldest known megalithic tombs date back over 8000 years ago, and can be found in Brittany in France. In Ireland on the top of the Ox Mountains, at Croaghaun, in Glen, another tomb has recently produced three carbon dates going back to around 5600BC.

At Carrowmore Megalithic Cemetery, Ireland, a date has recently been established for a tomb, said to be the oldest so far excavated in this area. The Carrowmore Cemetery is about 1,100 yards long and 700 yards wide. In this region there must have been a large settlement of people who had given up a nomadic way of life to live and work together as a large civilised community.

Many people have come here to study and carry out researches on these impressive stone structures. The Swedish Archaeological Excavations in 1979, and again recently in 1994, have established that the central cist and the boulder circle of Tomb 4 were built around 4800BC. One Swedish scholar, Goran Burenhult, has produced a brochure called *The Megalithic Cemetery of Carrowmore, Co. Sligo* where on page 5 he writes:

'The megalithic tradition died out 5000 years ago, so there is no traditional continuity, "or link", in Europe that can answer our questions, and we know almost nothing of the social, psychological and religious background that gave rise to them.'

Figure 3 *Carrowmore burial site.*

The author disagrees with this Swedish scholar as there had been continuity of our ancient indigenous culture which can be traced to the present time.

This belief by Burenhult is widely held by many people, and in this publication I will, with fresh eyes and open mind, attempt to readdress this commonly held view. Figure 3 illustrates the seal's head positioned centrally at the lower part of the stone as well as being shown at either end and also at the triangular shaped top of the stone. When viewing these stones it must be remembered that both weather and time have taken their toll of the clarity of these marvellous stone sculptures and rock art carvings.

In order to understand the sculptured rock art that has been carried out by the megalithic builders, it is necessary to stand back and look carefully at these monuments, or, better still, photograph and study them at leisure. It is also necessary to appreciate that these early people had a tremendous ability to inscribe one design on top of or beside another, thereby creating multi-shapes and designs within the same configuration. One of the first points to remember is, as earlier stated, that these early people held the whale in great regard and they considered the seal to be sacred.

Figure 4 *Megalithic dolmen, Carrowmore.*

They have incorporated the seal by either inscribed symbols or as a sculptured feature on many of these stones as part of their ceremonial ritual beliefs in a new life, and a new beginning after death.

When examining these stones, step back and look first at the overall shape of the stone, then look for triangles, as within the constructed triangle they may have created the face or the head of a seal. Figure 4 is a fine example of the large, triangular, wedge-shaped capstone being held aloft by the upright stones. At the right hand side of this wedge-shaped capstone is a triangular, stone composition representing the head of a seal with its small, incised, circular eye located two thirds of the way up from the bottom of this quoit. To the left of the first eye there is yet another eye almost on the same level which is highlighted by a diamond pattern sculptured in relief encompassing the circular eye; this is located almost in the middle of this photograph. Faintly inscribed between these two eyes is an obtuse angle, portraying the birth of the seal as if appearing from an open mouth formed by the obtuse angle. This to the Mesolithic people indicated the Beginning of life for the seal, and conversely they believed that man himself eventually evolved from the seal.

The inscribed angle forming the open aperture is also indicating one of the earliest symbols of Alpha. The letter 'A' forms an acute angle and can be referred to as a wedge shape, which to early man would have meant 'the beginning'. The left hand side of the stone is portraying the tapering tail of the whale/seal, from which another seal appears from the inscribed 150-degree obtuse angle; the seal head is highlighted by the deeper shadow of the pyramidal shape of the stone. The same seal, appearing on this truncated, triangular-shaped stone, has its eye looking downwards, its mouth appearing to rest on the lower inclined stone. The orthostats supporting the capstone have a 'V' shaped mouth located at the top of each stone, and also portray seal heads.

Figure 5 *New excavation at Carrowmore.*

Archaeologists at Carrowmore are currently excavating a dolmen, as shown in Figure 5. The top surface of the capstone has been triangularly shaped, with one side radiused. The stone shown in the foreground is also of a triangular shape, and on the top surface of this stone added in relief is a lozenge design, within which is an annulus also in relief. On all of these stones one can observe the faintly inscribed heads of seals. The stone in the centre is normally considered to be a blocking stone, thought to have been put in place when these early people had no further use for

the tomb. This stone was in fact positioned by the early people at the entrance to a chamber to indicate the transfer to the sky of the spirit of the departed.

A triangular design, similar to the top surface plan view of the quoit, appears around the eye of the seal, as can be observed on the inquisitive seal (Fig.6). Mesolithic people had studied the seal, and regarded it as a sacred creature, which transported the ancestral spirit of the deceased aloft to the heavens. They had carefully studied and recorded the many camouflaged designs found on the spotted body and head of the seal, and incorporated these patterns as sacred designs on ceremonial stones, in henges, portal tombs, round barrows, long barrows and stone circles. These same designs were to appear later in one of the earliest Christian churches in Rome.

Figure 6 *Inquisitive seal.*
By kind permission of Roderick Thorne.

The rounded head and eyes of seals were very important to the religious beliefs of early people. These religious convictions had been held for thousands of years, possibly even before the early Mesolithic Age, and can be traced down into the early Christian era. The symbol of a fish had been used by the early Christians in Greece, yet the symbol of sea-creatures had been used by the ancient people of Western Europe for many thousands of years before the Greeks became known for their scholarly learning. Carefully note the lozenge shape appearing around the seal's eye, and beyond to the clear triangular patch radiused similarly to the plan view of the quoit shown in Figure 5.

In Western Europe these prehistoric sepulchres were not haphazardly built and erected, but were carefully planned and supervised during construction. These stones were individually selected and sculptured to a high standard by craftsmen to a premeditated design and conception of the seal and the whale.

These sea-mammals have been inscribed and sculptured along with other symbols located within the portal stone structures. The basic foundation of many of these structures was based on an oval or elliptical pattern, which can be directly associated with the Vesica Piscis. The oval foundation also delineates the body of the seal, and this in turn has become known as a court tomb, or misleadingly as a horned tomb, similar to the Belas Knap Chambered Tomb, to be discussed further on in this chapter.

The large portal-tombs, popularly called 'dolmens', are normally single chamber tombs. The word 'dolmen' has come to be associated with these large, free-standing, megalithic chambers, where the portal-tomb comprises a chamber around which are placed predesigned orthostats in the general shape of a seal/whale. These stone orthostats represent seals/whales holding the capstone aloft to the heavens with their snouts, as shown by the Pentre Ifan Dolmen in Wales (Fig. 7). Pentre Ifan means Ivan's village, which overlooks the National Park of Pembrokeshire, and, in the distance, Cardigan Bay.

The Pentre Ifan Burial Chamber is one of the finest dolmens in Britain, and is located near the ferry-port of Fishguard. Once part of an ancient chambered tomb for the communal burial of the dead, it would have been in use for a great many years. It had been erected during the Neolithic Age, possibly long before 3500BC. The burial chamber had at one time been partially covered to form a long and large trapezoidal-shaped cairn, extending 120' in length to the rear of the structure. The large capstone, some 16' long, weighing over 16 tons, is supported by only three orthostats.

Excavations carried out in 1936–9, and again in1958–9, revealed that the burial chamber lay within a large oval pit, dug into the sloping ground, its sides originally constructed of dry stone walling. The forecourt area at the head of the structure had been carefully packed with stones. Until now it would appear that no one has commented on the impressive sculptured shapes appearing on this unique dolmen, especially that of a whale/seal being carried aloft by three seal/whale stone orthostats!

The blue stones, that had formed a ring and a 'U' shape within Stone-

Figure 7 *Pentre Ifan Dolmen.*

henge, had originally come from the Preseli Mountains, close to the Pentre Ifan Chamber. These stones would have been hauled to the nearest point on the Welsh coast and placed on rafts. They would then have been taken along the coast and floated up the Rivers Avon and Frome, in Somerset, to a landing site for transportation overland to Stonehenge.

The capstone of a dolmen or cromlech is known as a 'quoit', and, when viewed from different angles, can portray the heads of sea-creatures such as the whale, and the seal, and in some instances a combination of both. Some of the most striking examples of dolmens consist of only three up-rights supporting the sacred sea-creature capstone; this triangular con-figuration is referred to as a 'tripod-dolmen'. The triangle is a basic em-blem recognised by many early people in Western Europe as depicting the head of a seal. The front supports are normally taller than the rear single smaller support stone, inclining the capstone to a very intriguing and styl-ised position of the open mouth of a seal, while accentuating the entrance to the tomb.

To these early people the tomb represented two important ceremonial features, the Beginning and the End. The end had been inscribed as a diamond shape indicating the resting place of the dead, and later as a Neolithic symbol, the eyebrow of the seal, found on a lintel stone above

Figure 8 *Tapering seal body.*
By kind permission of Colin Baxter, Speyside

the S.E. cell of the Holm of Papa Westray chambered tomb in Orkney. The acute tapering angle of many of the quoits forms a wedge which represents 'A' for alpha, the beginning. The acute angle of the portal tomb structures and the wedge-shaped tombs can be traced to the tapering body of a seal, its head and its tail flipper, shown by the two seals on the rock (Fig. 8).

Observe how the wonderful camouflage of the seal's body merges with its acute tapering tail, appearing to look like the head of a sea-creature. Within this replica of a head there is a definite circular knuckle pattern imaging the bulging eye of a creature, with its mouth in this instance firmly closed. If one can envisage looking down on a plan view of this tail shape, it forms the basic design of a bishop's mitre. In other examples these bifurcating tail flippers can take on the form of a cluster of small seal heads similar to the photograph of the Basking Seal (Fig. 91). Moving up from the seal's tail, note the camouflaged formation of an angle as if it were an open mouth of another sea creature, from which a seal's head appears. A similar type of angle had been inscribed on the sculptured tail of the Kilclooney Dolmen (as shown on Colour Plate No. 15 and Fig. 17) illustrating another replica of the seal's head and eye. The apex of this angle is pointing directly to the inscribed circular eye, also indicating the ceremonial circle. Further lozenge patterns are clearly visible.

These markings on the seal, along with lozenge shapes of varying sizes are only some of the intriguing patterns and designs appearing and observed by early man as part of the seal's camouflage. These design patterns were copied and recopied and inscribed on their portal dolmens and other ceremonial burial sites. This acute angle shape of a seal's tail was looked upon as the beginning, from which the seal gave birth.

The two simple lines forming an acute angle inscribed on stone eventually became the letter 'A' representing the 'Beginning', and at a much later period became known as alpha. Early people believed that man himself had evolved from the seal, and in death they attempted to reincarnate the spirit of man in a new form of life as a seal. This allows us to understand how they viewed their tombs, which not only represented the 'End' of life, but to them a new 'Beginning' in life after death.

Various heads of the seal can appear at the sides and at the ends of a quoit, just as if two heads may appear, one at either end of a harbour, or spotted, seal's body (see Figs. 8,14 & 90). The Pentre Ifan Dolmen is of particular interest as several designs of heads of sea-creatures are to be found on all sides of this stone. The tapering shape of the stone is of a seal/whale depicted as giving birth to the seal. The overall shape and the camouflaged designs of the seal are easily observed at the tapering tail of the dolmen. This creation of a seal (Fig. 7) can be witnessed on this and other dolmen structures, wedge-shaped tombs, and menhirs, and on recumbent stones used in the formation of a stone circle. It is intriguing to note that many of the recumbent stones lying on the ground appear as if they are coming away from the burial complex, giving the impression of a sculptured stone seal moving away to a new-sprung life. This feature of recumbent stone seals moving away from a tomb has been found as a recurring feature on a great number of the megalithic sites discussed in this publication, and was an integral part of ancient man's ritual ceremonies for the deceased.

The eye of the whale/seal (Fig. 7) is seen looking towards the inclined head of the stone. Below this eye faintly depicted are two seals facing the head of the stone, as if swimming alongside the whale. Two thirds of the way along the quoit towards the tail is an open sculptured 'V' shape, shown lying on its side, from which a figure of a seal has emerged, indicating the 'beginning' of another sea-creature.

Sceptics will argue that the formation of this acute angle has been caused by the weathering of a thin layer of the stone; they may have a point, but when the design of this stone is studied in relation to the end view, then

Figure 9 *Rear view of Pentre Ifan.*

they may agree that this shape has been carefully sculptured, so that the quoit is angled slightly downwards in order to shed rainwater. The end view of the quoit, portraying a seal, has certain affinities to the seal perched on the rocks as shown on Figure 8.

The rear view of Pentre Ifan (Fig. 9) confirms that this quoit was sculptured intentionally. The left hand view shows the seal incorporated as an integral part of the design by the stone mason's deliberate removal of a layer of stone. The large orthostat on the left hand side, with several acute angles inscribed on it, is portraying the seal looking upwards. The face of this upright stone faintly shows frontal views of the head of the seal.

The orthostat in the foreground holding up the quoit has a crescent shape of the frontal view of a seal's head with its two large sculptured eyes peering out towards the bottom of the stone. The skull shape of this head is similar to the plan view of the capstone uncovered at Carrowmore, Ireland (Fig. 5) and to the patch found around the eye of the inquisitive seal (Fig. 6). In the socket of the right eye one can discern the outline of a small seal head with its mouth ajar. Further seal heads are also visible.

Figure 10 *The Overseer.*

The boulder in Figure 10 represents to me the Overseer of the Pentre Ifan Dolmen and shows the contra face of the stone imaged as the large boulder in the foreground of the Pentre Ifan Dolmen (Fig. 7). The overseer stone depicts the open, serrated mouth of possibly the whale, with a seal gently cradled within. During my research of the portal and wedge-shaped tombs it was observed that there is normally a large boulder positioned close by. This boulder may indicate another tomb, but it had been placed as if also witnessing the events of a ceremony for the departed and the subsequent transfer to a new life. Note the overseer peeking out in the background on Figures 7, 11, and 12.

On the other side of the dolmen (Fig. 11) one cannot fail to see on the quoit the heads of at least two sea-creatures, as if a whale and a seal are swimming in tandem. In the background just behind the single orthostat lies the recumbent form of a white stone, sculptured as a seal, and beyond to the left is the overseer boulder peering out keeping his weather eye on the ceremonial events taking place. The recumbent stones in the foreground also portray the seal in a very revealing way, as if representing the ancestral spirit of the deceased moving to a new beginning, 'A' – 'alpha'.

There are a great many seal head designs to be found on the quoit, orthostats, standing stones, and on several of the recumbent stones lying prostrate on the ground taking on the form of the seal on land. Of course the overseer, in conjunction with the other recumbent stones, played a significant role in the burial regeneration ceremonies, supervised by the high priest.

Figure 11 *Opposite side view of Pentre Ifan Dolmen.*

The tapering designed structure had been the basic framework for building the trapezoidal court-tomb, which portrays the body of the seal, with the court as the open mouth, indicating 'Omega' the 'end' and 'Alpha' as the 'beginning' in the form of spiritual regeneration. The formation of the three uprights is significant, as they form a simple isosceles triangle 'Delta', depicting the seal's head; also note the number of lozenge shapes appearing on these stones. The orthostats represent seals holding the capstone of the whale/seal aloft to the heavens above.

Looking at the end view of the head of the capstone (Fig. 12) the frontal view of the seal's head is observed, and again the side-views depict sea-creatures. The upright blocking-stone in the centre has a lozenge in relief depicted at the top, with its triangular apex pointing to the skies. Included within this lozenge is a triangle forming a further diamond shape with a small circle representing the eye and head of the seal, as shown on Figure 13. This upright blocking stone appears to have several combinations of the ancient symbols of 'Alpha' and 'Omega'.

Figure 12 *Pentre Ifan Dolmen blocking stone.*

The two standing stones to the right of the dolmen (Fig. 12) each depict a seal and the lozenge symbol highlighting the eye. Here on this monument are a number of examples showing a possible reason for the Phoenicians and the Greeks selecting 'A' for alpha, a simple symbol which had earlier been in common use throughout Europe, and may have spread with the building of dolmens throughout the Mediterranean and beyond.

The blocking stone, shown in Figure 12, illustrates in relief the lozenge shape with its symbolic design, as depicted on the seal (Fig. 14). Once again the all-seeing eye of the seal is highlighted. These people emphasised the eye of the seal incorporated within a lozenge and triangle pattern. Towards the end of this book I will attempt to illustrate how significant this symbol was to these early people, and its incorporation into our early Christian churches and our present day churches!

Small irregular saw-tooth shapes normally register water and waves, and the two waves or triangles as shown at the bottom of Figure 13 indicate the early symbol of 'omega', as illustrated by the shape of the eyebrows shown on the seal's head (Colour Plate 9). Later this symbol was to change to two rounded eyebrows similar to the small chalk Folkton drum (Fig. 65); again this design owes its origin to the eyebrow of the seal, which eventually became the symbol 'omega' meaning 'the end'. The eyebrow symbol also indicated the cell, or stall, in a passageway in which the remains of a person had been laid to rest.

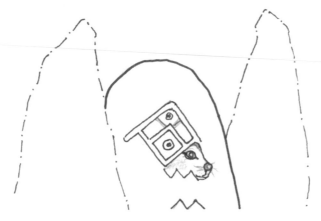

Figure 13 An early form of Alpha and Omega,

Ancient <u>Greek</u> & <u>Phoenician</u> 'A'

The Greek letter 'A' dates back to c.600BC, whereas the ancient people of Phoenicia and Canaan had a similar letter that may also have stood for the 'beginning' dating back to c.1700BC. Both Romans and Greeks considered that the letters of the alphabet had originated in the lands bordering the shores of the eastern Mediterranean, from among the Phoenicians, Egyptians, Assyrians, Cretans, and the Hebrews. The origin of 'A', 'W', 'X' and 'Z' symbols may have been based on earlier Mesolithic rock art attributes inscribed on megalithic tombs and stones found in Western Europe. These symbols can be traced to Britain, and Ireland, possibly before the Mediterranean people used them. The 'W' symbol alone can be traced back to the Neolithic period to c.3000BC in Ireland. Early people of Europe, living in the valleys of the Alps, were aware of these tall acute mountains, indicating 'A' the 'Beginning' and pointing the way to the heavens, to the beginning of a new life.

A recent publication *Journey Through The Ice Age*, by P.G.Bahn and J.Vertut, illustrates engravings on a huge block of schist located at Fornols-Haut, on a mountainside in the eastern French Pyrenees, at an altitude of 750m. These heads of animals are referred to as 'Stylistically they seem to belong to the Magdalenian'. From the photograph I recognise seal heads grouped in a similar manner to those rock carvings found in Northern Britain, and discussed here. The seal can be observed in other illustrations shown in *Journey Through The Ice Age*.

Figure 14 *Large lozenge design on body of seal.*
By kind permission of Roderick Thorne

These two playful seal pups (Fig. 14) are certainly of interest, as the one shown in the background has the large lozenge design located almost in the centre of its back, rather similar to the lozenge shape appearing on Figures 12 and 13. Within this equal-sided diamond pattern observed on the seal's body, the reader will note how the spotted camouflage illustrates a further pattern of other seal heads, with at least one head looking at the reader! There are many other acute angles with the eye depicted on this camouflaged body of the seal. Note how the tail end of the flipper of the white pup in the foreground appears as if it has another head to confuse predators, while the seal lying in the background looks very much like a common boulder found among the rocks on the seashore. In fact, if the large lozenge design appearing on the back of the seal in the background were inverted it would be almost an identical replica to that depicted on the blocking-stone (Figs. 12 and 13). Once again the triangular pattern appears around the eye of the seal shown in the foreground.

Returning down the path from Pentre Ifan, I noted the following cap-stone lying on top of a stone dyke running parallel to the path. This cap-stone appears to be inverted and has the sculptured shape of a seal. Seal heads are also visible at the side ends of this small quoit (Fig. 15).

As previously stated these megalithic structures should be viewed from a distance, and in fact were intended to be seen from the skies. Even when

Figure 15 *Upturned quoit near Pentre Ifan Dolmen.*

viewing a painting hung in an art-gallery it is normal practice to study and inspect the work of art at a distance in order to establish the finer details. The same principle applies, and even more so, when viewing these megalithic structures, as they were also intended to be seen and recognised instantly by the people of the tribe, and other travellers.

The importance of the seal can also be traced in Wales to a boy's Christian name, such as the Welsh 'Selwyn' meaning 'the beauty of a seal'. Some Welsh names for girls have been derived from the names of rivers in Wales. The heads of the rivers were directly associated with seals, as indicated by the megalithic triangle, the symbol later to be used by the Greeks in their alphabet as 'delta'. As part of their traditional dress Welsh ladies wore on their heads a tall black conical hat with a wide circular brim, similar to the hat associated with a witch and wizard. This custom may owe its origin to the long tapering body of the seal pointing upwards to the skies.

Hibernia

In the Northwest of Ireland, 4 miles from Ardara, on the moor behind the parish church at Kilclooney More, County Donegal, another truly impressive dolmen stands prominently against the skyline. The side view of the capstone had been carefully shaped and sculptured as a seal, readily verified by the photograph of this grand dolmen (Fig. 16).

Figure 16 *Kilclooney Dolmen.*

The capstone of the Kilclooney Dolmen is one of the most spectacular to be found in Ireland, weighing many tons, measuring nearly 20 feet in length. The design of the main seal portrays the creature's flippers as if it were swimming upwards to the sky. Obviously these early coastal people had an indepth understanding of the habit and lifestyle of the seal in the water.

Returning to the large head of the seal once again, as shown on the left hand side, it is interesting to observe the skill of the artist who had incorporated a second seal within this design, and the deep sculptured outline or scar that in turn forms the mouth of a whale. Carefully examine the outline once again, this time disregarding the seal, and in the centre towards the top of this stone focus on the larger eye of the whale! Again it is essential to look at these dolmen structures from a distance and from different angles in order to observe the other sculptured details of the seal and the whale on this stone monument.

What is so fascinating about this design is that the sculptured stone also represents two whale heads. The eye in the centre of the stone can look down to the acute angle, or in the opposite direction up towards the sky. The mouth of each creature is obvious on this incredible sculptured stone monument. Some people may liken the shape of this stone to that of a bird soaring to the sky. However, the importance of a bird located at a burial mound was associated with the Egyptians at a later period.

The top of the orthostat in Figure 16 provides a frontal view of the head of a seal, and one can observe the eyebrow and lozenge shapes near the top of the stone. The natural stone marking on this capstone is of particular interest, as it assists in confirming that early man spent a great deal of time searching, and finally selecting a suitably mottled stone to be sculptured.

The other side of this legendary monument (Fig. 17) depicts the seal as if swimming in the water with its flippers tucked into its body. The seal's head can be visualised not only at the top of the inclined capstone but also at the tail, where discerning readers will observe the inscribed angle along with another replica of the head and eye positioned towards the lower end of the capstone, as shown on the high definition close up view (Colour Plate 15). This is similar to the open 'V' shape of the angle as shown at the tail end of the seal on the rock (Fig. 8) and also as sculptured on the tail end of the Pentre Ifan Dolmen (Fig. 7).

Figure 17 *Side view of the Kilclooney Dolmen.*

Figure 18 *Soaring view of the Kilclooney Dolmen.*

Viewing Figure 18 I imagined the feelings of a defenceless skindiver swimming in the ocean depths, just as a large sea-creature glides effortlessly past, circling and wheeling inquisitively as if studying the struggling frame of humanity. This dolmen represents power that can readily overtake all obstacles before it. The right hand orthostat is a seal supporting the quoit with its snout. The symbol of the diamond complete with circle is found on the left hand orthostat. The acute apex of the diamond pattern points to the sky, the circular indentation within the diamond portraying the eye of the seal, while the diamond itself portrays the head. This diamond symbol also indicates the resting place of the dead.

Yet again there are two heads included within this soaring design, as seen on the right hand projection of this stone. The head of the first creature may be the head of a whale, and just below the eye is the inscribed shape of the seal swimming as if in parallel with the whale. The left hand view of this sculptured quoit is also that of a splendid sea-creature. On the underside of some of these dolmen capstones one can also find further inscribed seals' heads.

Figure 19 *Kilclooney Overseer.*

On the way back down from the moor, on the left hand side of the peat track, a further boulder was found not too far from the dolmen. This to me was the 'Overseer' for the Kilclooney Monument. Again the head of a sea-creature was observed, as shown on Figure 19.

Here on the path surrounded by ferns and brushwood a b
out to portray multi-heads of the seal and the whale, shaped l
The head of the whale is clearly visible cradling a seal within it
The head of the whale looks over this wild and desolate moo
one time had been home to a thriving community, bustling a
everyday chores, and paying homage to their ancient ancestors.

Southern England is famous for the outline of the well
Uffington White Horse, in Oxfordshire, and for the Cerne Abba
in Dorset. The outlines of these figures have been cut out of the
hills to be seen not only from a distance at ground level but, as in
intended, to be seen from the sky by their heavenly gods. This same
ciple applies to the chamber tombs, such as the plan view of Belas K
where the aerial photograph shows the outline of the seal with its mo
wide open at the northern end.

Belas Knap Chambered Tomb

The Portal Dolmen structures were the skeletal framework for the entrance to a Court Tomb. A dry stone construction was built around the trapezoidal foundation, then covered over with soil to form the body shape of the seal, as seen at Belas Knap Chambered Tomb. Belas Knap is situated on top of the Cotswold Hills, near the quaint picturesque village of Winchcombe in Gloucestershire. This ancient monument is 183 feet long, 60 feet wide, and 13 feet high at the north end, where it has a false entry referred to as having a horned forecourt. The general shape of this tomb is of a half tubular cross section forming a long, tapering trapezoidal mound. The south end of the mound has a definite forecourt, said to be positioned between two projections or 'horns'. Over the centuries the reference to horns by academics has been highly misleading and has resulted in misguiding scholars as to the true nature and significance of these tombs.

The mound of Belas Knap has a long, low outline forming a sweeping curve, as if it were a sea-creature gently breaking the surface of the water. This is exactly what our Neolithic ancestors wanted to portray. When looked at from the air, the overall shape of this long mound resembles the

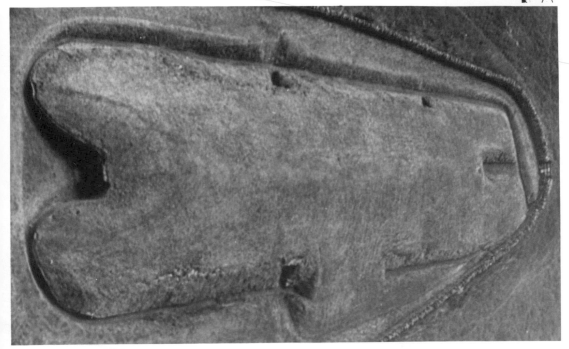

Figure 20 *Aerial View of Belas Knap Chambered Tomb.*
By kind permission of Cambridge University Collection of Air Photographs: copyright reserved

outline of a seal with its mouth open and swimming on its side. The tomb entrance at the bottom of the figure is placed beside the seal's flipper partly cut-off. The tomb entrances at the top represent the eyes of seals, one with its mouth open as positioned looking to the left, while the second entrance indicates an eye of a seal looking to the right with its mouth ajar. The southern corridor is indicated by the pronounced twin tail flippers of the seal. Figure 21 illustrates a seal with its tail splayed in an open 'V' formation.

Figure 21 *'V' shaped flippers of the seal.*

Stone Age Alpha

Two passages face the east, while another faces the west. The east-facing passages are aligned to the sun's rays rising over the hills, allowing a shaft of light to enter the chamber at the break of dawn, whereas the west chamber passage catches the last glimmer of light from the sun as it sinks in the western skies. This is another valuable reason for locating these tombs on the tops of hills. The main dates for the sunrise ceremonies at Belas Knap were 21st March, during the spring equinox, and 21st September, during the autumn equinox.

In one chamber it was interesting to trace the very *faint* shape of the seal, and also a 'V' shape symbol incised on a stone in the passageway, similar to the arrow symbols found on the symbol stones in Northern Britain. Whilst taking a photograph in this chamber, I was delighted to find the head of a bull-seal positioned at the right hand side of the chamber (Fig. 22). This head is, I believe, a form of Neolithic mosaic rock art, the artwork having been created by the positioning of the stones as a mosaic pattern on the wall of the corbelled stone chamber. These corbelled stones also portray in their own right heads of seals.

Figure 22 *Stone wall mosaic art.*

A female seal appears to cower timidly behind the bull-seal head, and another is seen at the rear left hand side of the chamber between the 'V' of two recumbent stones, confirming the ability of these early artists to create a design on top of or within the shape of the original design; a number of other seal heads are located around the head of the bull-seal, shown as if they are striving to get out of the tomb. The bull-seal appears to be guarding both the tomb and the female seals, its mouth fashioning a menacing snarl at those daring to enter this sacred chamber. Across the top of the prominent recumbent stone in Figure 22 is a seal with arched back lying stretched out looking to the left.

The corbel stones may have been coloured, with the head of the bull-seal only a fragment of the art which had at one time appeared on these corbelled stone walls. Further mosaic shapes are seen along with a crude form of a triangular framed outline design on the corbelled walls, shown a little more clearly on Colour Plate No.1. Seals' heads can be seen at the right hand side of Figure 23, traced at either end of the recumbent stones and also portrayed on the surface of the other stones.

Figure 23 Outline of corbelled wall design.

Trusty's Hill Symbolic Boulder

The threatening pose of the bull-seal in the Belas Knap Chamber is strikingly similar to the inscribed figure of a bull-seal bellowing his challenge to intruders attempting to approach the ancient hillfort, at the top of Trusty's Hill, Gatehouse of Fleet, on the Solway Firth.

Figure 24 *Ancient boulder symbols.*

Professor Charles Thomas recorded in his book, *The Early Christian Archaeology of North Britain*, (1986), that the inscribed figure on the right hand side of the boulder refers to an 'S' type dragon! I understand what he is attempting to say. However, when Professor Thomas has time to reflect and to study the seal as referred to, he may now agree that the Bull-Seal is a suitable identity for the 'S' type mammal. The Bull-Seal is rearing itself on a spiral tail of vitality and life, as if to protect its harem of female seals by pursing its mouth to bellow out a warning to all intruders to this ancient hillfort of the Solway Seal Tribe.

Figure 25 *Seal exhaling.*

Figure 25 shows a seal with its lozenged eye emerging from the water for air, pursing its mouth to a shape similar to the bull-seal's mouth depicted on the boulder rock at Trusty's Hill. Recently on a new megalithic site I came across a very large boulder sculptured as a seal's head, again with its mouth shaped similarly to that of the bull-seal on the Trusty's Hill Boulder.

On the right hand side of the boulder at Trusty's Hill is the inscribed shape of a ceremonial dagger, with its blade pointing to the heart of the bull-seal, emphasising that the origin of the tribe can be linked directly to the seal. This ceremonial dagger delineates the body shape of a seal and is the plan view of the nearby Cairnholy I Chambered Tomb. The ceremonial, circular handle-face, depicting the mouth and eyes of a seal, in turn portrays the semi-circular facade of Cairnholy I formed by eight upright stones, which themselves represent stone images of stretching upright seals as if offering this tomb and its contents to the heavens.

Directly behind the circle of the ceremonial blade is the shape of another seal's head, the eye of which can look both inwards or outwards. By taking our gaze along the length of the blade the sculptor highlights the importance of the bull-seal to the tribe. Drawing attention to the bull-seal in this way indicated the origin of the tribe and the relevance of their spiritual beliefs. Ceremonial daggers can be seen inscribed on boulders and menhirs throughout Europe, including Stonehenge, and may also indicate plan views of other burial chambers in the area.

One female seal is intertwined with the lower area of the ' Z'-Rod (Fig. 26) and is positioned on the left hand side of the upright bull-seal whose snout is just visible in the top right-hand corner of the boulder. Figure 26 portrays some of the intriguing symbols that appear on many of Scotland's symbol stones, many of which date back to the Bronze Age or to an even earlier period. The fascinating double disc bisected by the 'Z'- rod is in its own right a creative work of art which has puzzled people for many centuries. The double disc may represent a double ceremonial henge, linked by an avenue, or even relate to two round barrows.

Some indigenous inhabitants of the Island of Skye have referred to the double disc symbols as bespectacled eyes! They were not far wrong, as these designs are directly related to the all-seeing eyes of the seal. The early people who inhabited our shores were obsessed by the seal and its sheer liveliness in the water. They were aware of the presence of inquisitive seals, as the triangular heads and the eyes frequently surfaced out of the water to survey what humans were up to on their territorial coastal shore.

The double disc bisected by the 'Z'-rod may at a later date have had the decoration added to what had been a plain inscribed 'Z'-rod, indicating the ceremonial breaking in two of the war lance, announcing the tribe's acceptance of a new faith, and a new beginning. Older and simpler 'V'

symbols appearing on this rock may confirm the later addition of the decoration to the 'Z'-Rod.

Figure 26 *Seal and 'Z'-rod.*

Between the double disc and the lower broken part of the war lance is
the shape of a female seal, with the folds of her skin clearly shown on the
underside of her neck. The seal appears as if swimming away to the left,
attended by small fish formed by the lappets of the war lance. The tail end
of the seal, at the acute angle, forms a figure of a sea-creature, again similar to that of the seal on the rocks (Fig. 8). Several other triangles had been
inscribed at a much earlier period, all with the head of the seal within the
acute angles, the largest of which forms a large 'V' pointing to the ground,
its apex almost in the centre, slightly below the lower leg of the 'Z'- rod.

In my book *The Message of Scotland's Symbol Stones*, I briefly mentioned Trusty's Hill, and Cairnholy I and II. Finding further confirmation of the religious beliefs of the early people from Belas Knap and Pentre Ifan led me back to re-evaluate Cairnholy I and II, enabling me to establish other important links between the seal tribe of Trusty's Hill and the stone structures of Cairnholy I and II in the Solway Firth.

Figure 27 *Semi-circular facade of Cairnholy I.*

The recumbent stone positioned within the centre of the semicircular facade (Fig. 27) is portraying a seal as if it had emerged from the long tapering mound representing the tomb of the mother seal. Cairnholy I and II are located about 5 miles from Trusty's Hill. These ceremonial burial sites are referred to as 'Clyde' cairns, although they deviate slightly from the 'classic' style of the Clyde cairns. This type of cairn is normally trapezoidal in shape with the main chamber leading from the crescent-type forecourt, representing the open mouth of the seal. This is a development of the Court Tombs, smaller and less elaborate than the Belas Knap Chamber Tomb. These pillar stones are all representing seals, some having an inscribed 'V' shaped type mouth; one such stone is positioned to the right of the recumbent stone lying to the left (Fig. 28). This recumbent seal stone, although smaller, is uncannily similar to the side view of the capstone found perched on the Pentre Ifan Dolmen, Wales (Fig. 7).

Figure 28 *Rear View of Cairnholy I Mound.*

The narrow stone pinnacle shown on the far right is the shape of a seal's head and body, this body outline itself sculptured as a side view of a snout of a larger head of a seal, looming from the open inscribed 'V' mouth towards the base of the stone. There are other heads shown on this interesting stone. At the bottom right hand corner of this photograph are a number of smaller stone boulders representing the eye and the snout of a seal. The other pillars also portray seals standing upright with heads raised in a beckoning fashion to the skies. A smaller stone placed to the left of the tallest pillar illustrates a seal facing forward.

The inclined side view of the capstone of Cairnholy II (Fig. 29) indicates the open mouth of the seal forming the acute angle representing the beginning. Directly behind the quoit is the tall pillar stone, raised as if it were the tapering tail of the seal pointing upwards to the empyrean, with the two smaller upright stones indicating the rising of an individual's soul to the firmament.

There are many other smaller sculptured heads of seals scattered around on these mounds. The present day custom of hill-walkers carrying a stone to place on top of a cairn may owe its origin to early people carrying a stone sculptured as a seal or the head of a seal and placing it on the cairn as a memorial to their departed ancestor.

Figure 29 *Cairnholy II chamber.*

Re-examining Cairnholy II, it occurred to me that the recumbent stone lying on the ground under the capstone may have been considered by early man as a sculptured seal emerging as the regenerated spirit of the dead from under the shadow of the circular capstone, which forms the acute angle delineating the beginning. The right-hand orthostat represents a seal holding up the quoit as if to allow the recumbent seal to emerge from the shadows. The single stone to the right of the picture is intended to be a seal which had emerged earlier, with its snout held high as if sniffing and tasting the air for the first time whilst it surveys all before it.

On the lower area of Trusty's Hill boulder a small inscribed circle with two rising spirals (not shown) refers to the circular capstone of Cairnholy II cairn, the rising spirals indicating the spiritual rising of the deceased.

The eye and the head of the seal encompassed within the double 'V' shape design can clearly be determined on the furthest away orthostat to the rear of this quoit (Fig. 29). The tallest orthostat is also portraying a seal emerging, similar to the pinnacle stone of Cairnholy I (Fig. 27).

Careful examination of the top of the capstone revealed to my delight that it had been shaped at the rear end as the large head of a seal, as illustrated on the right hand side of Figure 30.

The weathered eye, snout and open mouth of this splendid sculptured head are highlighted by its shadow and that of the sculpted orthostat, which has the acute angle for 'A'- alpha shown in relief and depicts the birth of a seal, a new life emerging from the tomb.

Figure 30 *Seal head at the rear of the quoit.*

Southwest England

Turning now to the Southwest of England, with its long established trading links with the coastal dwellers of Scotland's west coast, the meaning and understanding of why these enigmatic dolmens, standing stones and circles were erected on the moors of Cornwall and Devon have been lost in time. Today they are looked upon as great unsolved mysteries, holding a deep fascination for the many thousands of tourists who visit them in their scenic upland surroundings.

Figure 31 *Trethevy Dolmen, Cornwall.*

The steeply inclined capstone of Trethevy Dolmen, in Cornwall, portrays a quoit forming an acute angle or a wedge-shape symbol indicating 'The Beginning'. In the area where my wife is looking at the orthostat, there is also an open angle, only one of many 'alpha' symbols very faintly observed on this dolmen.

The orthostat directly behind my wife portrays the frontal head view of the seal, as does the closing orthostat with its radius corner, shown at the right hand side of the photograph. This stone along with the end view of the quoit are both inscribed with the 'alpha' symbol and the lozenge design.

Figure 32 Men-Scryfa Symbol Stone.

In the Old Testament the story of the whale has played a major role in the beliefs of these early people, which eventually progressed to Christianity. The other sea mammal, the seal, had also been relevant to Neolithic peoples' religious beliefs, which were adopted and accommodated by the early Christian Church; the shape of the Bishop's mitre used even today is a simple example of adopting the beliefs and customs of early man.

The Men-Scryfa Symbol Stone is located near Penzance, Cornwall. This symbol stone has attracted scholars to study the Roman inscriptions, yet academics have been unaware that this stone had been carefully designed and sculptured as a symbolic figure indicating the Beginning of Life.

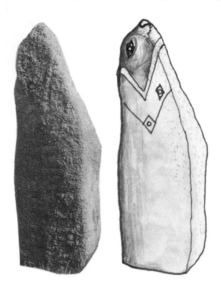

Figure 33 Birth of a seal.

The Men-Scryfa Symbol Stone is another fundamental record of the aspirations and the culture of ancient man, who had included in the design the sculptured figures of the seal and the whale. My first thought on looking at the overall shape of the stone was that the whale was swallowing the seal. However, early man had been portraying his belief in the evolution of man as related to the whale and the seal, believing that the seal created by the whale was then brought ashore in its mouth to enable the seal to live on land as well as in the sea. (cf. The story of Jonah swallowed by the whale, then returned safely to land.)

The sketch in Figure 33 has been shown to highlight ill-defined detail on this menhir, ignoring the Roman lettering in order to concentrate on the seal as if being disgorged by the whale. Colour Plate No.3 illustrates the open mouth more clearly and confirms that photographing these stones must be carried out at a particular time of day, and even time of year, in order to establish the true shadow highlighting the symbols appearing on these stones. The open orifice can also be faintly seen on the other side of this menhir, as in Figure 32.

A further outline of an inscribed acute angle is positioned below the open sculptured aperture representing the birth of a seal. Here is an early attempt to portray the sculptured creation of the seal with a symbol, which later became known as alpha, but to them meant the beginning of life after death (confirmed by the small lozenge shape appearing within the acute angle).

Taking the photograph of the Men-Scryfa Stone (Fig. 32) I realised that the stone would have been centrally positioned in relation to the centralised hollow of the interesting hill in the background. Unfortunately time did not allow me to carry out an inspection of this fascinating hill, where the cup shape may have been dug out by Mesolithic man, with the contour of the hill on either side of this cup shape taking on the form of seal heads as if witnessing the events on the moor below.

A few hundred yards further down the hill from the Men-Scryfa Stone is the impressive ringed Men-an-Tol Stone (Cornish: maen = stone; tol = hole). This holed stone is best described as a stone in the form of hexagonal annulation, which may also confirm the origin of the saltire emblem 'X'. The group of stones stand in a gorse-fringed clearing just off the main moorland track in an open landscape of peat and moor.

A seal is faintly perceived lying prostrate on top of the left hand face of the inclined edge of the perimeter of the hexagon; directly below this lies another seal with its head formed by the obtuse angle of the hexagon shape, its head facing outwards. The two standing stones also represent the 'overseer' seals, and the deeply carved shape of the acute angle representing 'A' for alpha cut into the upright stone in the background indicates the open mouth of the seal, just as the mouth of the seal was emphasised at Belas Knap Chambered Tomb. The frontal view of the head of the seal with its eyes located above the orifice on the stone, its mouth open, formed by the circular hole, also relates to the 'Beginning'.

The recumbent stone in the foreground has several seal heads facing to the right and one facing to the left. This alignment of stones again testifies to the beliefs of early man and his role in assisting the dead to pass through this aperture to a new life after death, linked to the sacred seal; the interesting recumbent seal-shaped stones may testify to this new spiritual role.

Figure 34 *Men-an-Tol-Stones.*

The Men-an-Tol-Stones had been documented in c.1700 by Thomas Tonkin, who noted that these stones had been associated through the ages with people who came here for cures for a variety of ailments; healing and fertility rites were held, as people squeezed their bodies through the circular hole under the shadow of these fascinating stones. The Mesolithic people may have passed the skeletal remains of the dead through this orifice, witnessed by the upright seal overseer stones. Many holed stones are to be found in this area, and indeed throughout Europe. In Belgium, there is a holed orthostat on the Dolmen at Hérault, and on the Dolmen at Constans, in France. In Ireland, the Poulnabrone Dolmen is well documented and much photographed, but in the vicinity of this dolmen there is a less well-known 'D' shaped holed stone.

Figure 35 *Poulnabrone Holed Stone.*

In Co.Clare, north-west Ireland, only 5 miles south of Ballyvaughan in the limestone uplands known as the Burren, where lies the rich habitat of an exceptional variety of fauna, rare Alpine and Mediterranean plants thrive in the fissures of limestone rock. This is a strange land of surface pavements of limestone weathered in an extraordinary manner, producing characteristic deeply fluted patterns known as Karren. This is the stark setting for the Poulnabrone Holed Stone and the more famous weathered Poulnabrone Dolmen.

The 'D' shaped hole of this upright hexagonal saltire type ceremonial stone faces the nearby Poulnabrone Dolmen. In the left hand corner of the photograph (Fig. 35) there is the silent figure of a sculptured seal, expectantly waiting and watching as the overseer for the next sequence in the regeneration ceremony to take place.

On this stone several heads of seals are observed, one with its eyes positioned just above the opening of the 'D'. Looking from the 'D' shaped holed stone to the orthostats of the Dolmen reveal the faint images of large heads of seals appearing on these upright pillars.

Figure 36 Poulnabrone Dolmen.

This tapering portal tomb is recognised instantly by one of its many sculptured profiles; my photograph may well be one of the lesser known views. Note the overseer stone of the seal viewed in the distance between the two orthostats, positioned closer to the upright orthostat on the left The end view of the dolmen depicts the shape of the head and eye of a whale, about to swim past with its mouth slightly ajar, and other sculptured heads, this time of seals, as if swimming along side one another. These heads are located just above and along the top lip of the mouth of the whale; these, I agree, do appear faintly on the reproduced photograph. To the left of this capstone heads of several seals protrude along the inclined tapering edge. The large frontal view of the head of a seal is faintly imaged on the side of the left hand orthostat.

A smaller secondary quoit positioned closer to the ground has a variety of heads of sea-creatures appearing on its edges. In the foreground and around this monument are scattered many stones forming sculptured heads of seals, memorials to the dead left by their descendants. It becomes evident that the manufacture of these scattered stone heads was once part of a thriving economy, employing many people to sustain the ever-growing demand for the supply of sculptured stone seals, or merely heads, as memorials to the departed.

Wedge-Shaped Tombs

While researching in the Burren area it was interesting to examine some of the many burial chambers known as wedge-shaped gallery graves. These were built as a simplification of the labour-intensive dolmen. The wedge-shaped grave (Fig. 37) is one of the most interesting and revealing of these chambers. The capstone portrays the head of a whale on the left, while on the right it represents a seal. On the lower section of the capstone there are many other heads of seals; one positioned on the left hand side in the forefront has its mouth open, and the seal behind and positioned with its head in front of the other has its mouth closed.

The wedge-shaped tombs differ from the portal tombs by having the orthostats placed on their side in a tandem tapering formation, hence the name wedge. This wedge-shape also depicts an open mouth or entrance to the tomb. The lower position of the stones has helped to safeguard the artwork on these stones from the weather, and in turn has protected one of the finest portrayals of a seal's head so far found in my research. This is highlighted by the natural colouring of the stone as it matches the shading and the marking of a large seal head. The head positioned near the centre is depicted on the right hand supporting stone and has been portrayed as having the same depth as the inner tandem stone, where the eye is looking out to the foreground, and is as clear as if it had been shaped yesterday, as is the detail of the head, mouth and the snout, located closer to the ground (Fig. 37).

Figure 37 *Wedge-shaped burren tomb.*

This fabulous figure of a seal's head can take on both a frontal and side view of the seal, and as a work of rock art it is quite remarkable, even although the top surface of the quoit has been extensively weathered. Examine also Colour Plate No.2, showing this photograph yet again, as to me this is a unique art-form that has gone unnoticed through the passage of time, well protected in this instance from the elements.

The recumbent orthostat support stone to the left illustrates a roughly-shaped seal's head with a serrated mouth. The side view of the quoit, as illustrated, has a number of seal heads depicted.

Our next wedge-shaped tomb (Fig. 38) is referred to as Parknabinnia, close to the village of Kilnaboy. Directly across the narrow road from this gallery grave stands a roundish boulder (not illustrated), a seal's head with its mouth open, the overseer for this tomb.

Figure 38 *Wedge-shaped gallery grave.*

The head of the seal can readily be recognised at either end of the Parknabinnia capstone; on the capstone and on the supports further heads can also be seen from various angles as one circumvents the tomb. The end view, as illustrated, is the smaller opening, whereas the side directly opposite shows a wider and higher entrance to the chamber. These chambers were often surrounded by several low walls and a cairn created around them by mourners, by the addition of sculptured heads of stone seals, as witnessed among many of the stones scattered around this sacred area.

Wedge-shaped Gallery Graves are the commonest form of megalithic tombs found in the Burren, and date from the late Neolithic and Early Bronze Age, 2000–1400 BC.

Haroldstown Dolmen

The Haroldstown Dolmen, County Carlow, had been used by a family as their home during the 19th century. More spacious than most this portal dolmen stands near the bank of the River Derreen and the crossroads at the Bridge of Acuan. The chamber is 13 feet long, and at its widest 9 feet. Some people have described it as having two capstones. The larger top quoit is the main capstone, whereas the smaller inclined stone to the left may be described as the 'overseer', with its eye just visible as it noses into the inner chamber. This stone may have been located a short distance away, and brought closer to the main chamber either by farmers or the people who had turned the space within the chamber into a home.

Figure 39 *Haroldstown Dolmen.*

What has particularly interested me is the number of heads of seals inscribed on this capstone, especially those showing a frontal view of a seal's head. These are positioned along the length of the quoit. On the right hand side of the quoit are the heads of two seals appearing as if from an obtuse angle; this angle is basically similar to the one shown at the tail end of the seal (*see* Fig. 8).

The other orthostats also have faintly inscribed shapes of the seal incorporated within these uprights, as does the lozenge shaped stone. The orthostat on the right has two diamond patterns cut in relief, within which is an inscribed circle indicating the eye of a seal looking upwards at the capstone it is supporting; also observe the acute triangle, shown at the left hand side of this stone, indicating the 'beginning'.

Near the top of the inclined stone on the left a diamond shape is seen faintly in the area shadowed by the quoit (Fig. 39). This again portrays the head and eye of a seal, and the 'V' shape formation from which other heads appear. These early people have copied the camouflaged body of the seal and incorporated this into their religious rituals and ceremonies.

Figure 40 *Kilmogue Dolmen.*

Another remarkable dolmen is the well-known Kilmogue Dolmen at Kilkenny. The angle of this quoit is steep as it reaches out supported by two orthostats, while its tail is resting on top of a smaller capstone. The shape of this monument clearly represents the open mouth, 'A' for the 'Beginning'.

The head, mouth and eye of the seal are seen quite clearly at the top of this inclined stone. A further eye of a seal can be observed a quarter way down from the top and nearer to the top surface of the capstone as if looking to the top of the quoit. Readers should note that the constructed triangle in the centre of this inclined stone has its sides gently curved, with the head of a seal looking towards the tail. This curved triangle, an important emblem used by early man to indicate the head and eye of the seal, was later to become the basic design of the gable walls and rafters supporting the roofs of early Christian churches, and may well be the true origin of European Gothic design, which then led to the overall shape for the heraldic banner.

The orthostat has several heads of seals shown on this upright stone, some near the bottom, and one three feet up from ground level and to the right, with two others just above looking to the right. There is also a large frontal view of the head of a seal half way up towards the centre of this supporting stone. The general shape of the orthostats also represents the seal.

The recumbent stone to the bottom left hand side has also been sculptured in relief. The large head of a seal is shown at the top right hand corner of this recumbent stone; from the head follow the body shape to the centre of this stone to reveal a very faint outline of another seal's head with its eye clearly enclosed within a lozenge design. Moving along to the end of the stone we find several heads of seals. Close to the grass is another upturned head of a seal. If this recumbent stone were turned to an upright position the overall shape would be that of an orthostat representing the seal. Recumbent stones were incorporated among the periphery stones enclosing the Passage Grave, Newgrange, Southern Ireland.

The Neolithic period had been a dynamic time for people, with changes in trading and social structures, as well as the simplification of burial practices whereby recumbent stones saved many man-hours and the effort of hoisting large stones to a vertical position. The change in religious thinking introduced a continuous ring of recumbent stones positioned as if welcoming the recent dead to their midst.

Guernsey Channel Island Connection

The Men-Scryfa Symbol Stone may also be a development from a Menhir found among the many tombs and stones on the enchanting island of Guernsey. This Menhir, known as 'Le Dehus', has very odd markings, as if illustrating the sculptured gills of a large sea-creature.

Figure 41 *'Le Dehus' Menhir.*
By kind permission of G.Rankin

Indeed this was exactly what the ancient coastal dwellers of the island had intended, as this symbolic standing stone (Fig. 41) is representing a sea-creature, possibly a whale. There are several other symbols which can be observed in this photograph; at the top of the stone is the sculptured head of a seal which seems to have just surfaced from the water; and in front of the seal's snout it creates a small wake, as it slowly swims forward gently disturbing the water in which appear to be several smaller heads of seal pups, a symbol of creation and rebirth.

The photograph taken inside 'Le Dehus' chamber (Fig. 42), is most revealing, and a further photograph, Colour Plate No.5, is illustrated in this book to highlight this remarkable burial chamber. This site owes its preservation to John De Havilland who in 1775 purchased it from quarrymen.

Figure 42 *'Le Dehus' Burial Chamber.*
By kind permission of G. Rankin

The top of the central symbol stone indicates the beginning of a new life in the form of a seal representing the regeneration of the deceased spirit. The orthostat on the left hand side has been inscribed with large lozenge patterns, similar to those shown in the foreground of Colour Plates No.11 and 12.

All the orthostats are indicating seals supporting the stones which form the roof; these orthostats also have faint images of multi-seal heads incised on them. The two orthostats on the left have each a good view of the head of a seal at the base of the stone, also observed on Colour Plate No.5.

Figure 43 *Vale Stones, Guernsey.*
By kind permission of G.Rankin

The stone on the left of the photograph (Fig. 43) is showing the weathered sculptured shape of a seal head, the overseer, looking to the left into the gorse. There are several more seal heads, not as clearly defined.

Many legends abound in Scotland of seals coming ashore and removing their skins, hiding them in crevices among the rocks, as they take on the form of beautiful maidens. These transformed creatures are said to have sung and danced on the shore to attract the attention of unwary fishermen. Some married these unsuspecting fisher-folk and bore their children; they then became known as 'seal people'.

These stories can be traced back through time to the indigenous people of Western Europe. In Orkney the seals are known as 'Selkies', and the people of Orkney refer to an even later group of people known as 'Fin folk', who paddled around these islands in their kayaks, discarding their seal skins as they came ashore. It does appear that the people of Orkney had at one time controlled and governed Scotland, and may have derived their Orcadian name from Orca, the killer whale, which still hunts the migratory shoals of fish and seals around our northern islands. Our ancient ancestors from Western Europe were responsible for carrying their ancient mythical seal stories to the seafaring Phoenicians, who may have retold them to the people of the Mediterranean.

Another mythical character originating from the seal stories is the mermaid. One, made famous by Hans Christian Andersen, can be seen in Denmark, at the entrance to the harbour of Copenhagen, where ships sail past the statue of the Little Mermaid. However, from Cornwall, comes the grand, old story of The Mermaid of Zennor.

The Mermaid of Zennor

"Hundreds of years ago a very beautiful and richly attired lady attended service in Zennor Church occasionally - now and then she went to Morvah also; her visits were by no means regular - often long intervals would elapse between them.

Yet whenever she came the people were enchanted with her good looks and sweet singing. Although Zennor folks were remarkable for their fine psalmody, she excelled them all; and they wondered how, after the scores of years that they had seen her, she continued to look so young and fair. No one knew from whence she came nor whither she went; yet many watched her as far as they could see from Tregarthen Hill.

She took notice of a fine young man, called Mathey Trewella, who was the best singer in the parish. He once followed her, but he never returned; after that she was never seen more in Zennor Church, and it might not have been known to this day who or what she was but for the merest accident.

One Sunday morning a vessel cast anchor about a mile from

Pendower Cove; soon after a mermaid came alongside and hailed the ship. Rising out of the water as far as her waist, with her yellow hair floating around her, she told the captain that she was just returning from church, and requested him to trip his anchor just for a minute, as the fluke of it rested on the floor of her dwelling, and she was anxious to get in to her children.

Others say that while she was out on the ocean a-fishing of a Sunday morning, the anchor was dropped on the trapdoor which gave her access to her submarine abode. Finding on her return, how she was hindered from opening her door, she begged the captain to have the anchor raised that she might enter her dwelling to dress the children and be ready in time for church.

However it may be, her polite request had a magical effect on the sailors, for they immediately worked with a will, hove anchor and set sail, not wishing to remain a moment longer than they could near her habitation. Seafaring men, who understood most about mermaids, regarded their appearance as a token that bad luck was near at hand. It was believed that they had often lured men to live with them.

When Zennor folk learned that a mermaid dwelt near Pendower, and what she had told the captain, they concluded that it was this sea-lady who had visited their church and enticed Trewella to her abode. To commemorate these somewhat unusual events they had the figure she bore - when in her ocean home - carved in holy-oak, which may still be seen." (Bottrell 1873, p.288. Ian McNeil Cooke, 1993.)

The side of the wooden carved seat of the mermaid from Zennor Parish Church (Fig. 44) is of significant interest, as the mermaid is holding up a mirror in one hand and a comb in the other. The symbol of the comb and the mirror can be traced back to the ancient Symbol Stones of Scotland, and directly to the Bronze Age period in Britain.

Figure 44 *Mermaid, Zennor Parish Church.*

The comb has always represented personal cleanliness, and was used for cleaning and teasing wool prior to spinning. It also held a religious significance attributed to the existence of a ritual cleansing taking place at a cairn or cist, located close to the larger stone circle and its smaller satellite circle. A symbol of achievement in a community, it was linked to the religious, spiritual faith of the worshipper. It is conceivable that the hand-mirror was a symbol of personal development designed from the religious philosophy of worshippers paying homage at stone circles, whereby the mirror portrayed the plan view of a large stone circle with its avenue linked to a smaller satellite circle. The stone circle was looked upon as a mirror, reflecting their faith to the heavens.

Figure 45 *Bronze mirror from Desborough.*

The intricate Bronze Age hand-mirror, found at Desborough, North-amptonshire, is one of the most exciting decorated artefacts known today in Britain. This hand-mirror has been illustrated in books, yet no one to date, as far as I am aware, has been able to interpret these interesting, flowing designs presented on the back of this bronze mirror.

The back of the mirror can be inverted to display further seals, encom-passing the large head of a seal within which is a three quarter size head, with a still smaller head of a seal, positioned almost in the centre of the mirror. The detail of the smaller head will enable the reader to under-stand the artist's build-up to these lively, frolicsome scenes of seals at play in the sea.

The sheer brilliance of the ancient artist is mind-boggling, as he por-trays many swift-moving seals darting rapidly here and there through the water. The artwork of the Gael can be traced to this lively movement of the seal moving acrobatically in his own environment. From Mesolithic

times and possibly even earlier the emphasis had always been placed by early people on the wonderful eyes, mouth, and circular head of the seal. These energetic creatures were an integrated part of their social culture, economy and religious outlook, a way of life that had been established as the very heart of their ancient stone society, which may reach back further than we can envisage.

Looking once more at these symbolic cult figure-heads of the seal, one can determine that the pair of eyes represented a set of Round Barrows and that the mouth was the centre of their ceremonial rituals within a circular henge. Round Barrows were placed as a pair either within or out-with a circular henge. The Round Barrow replaced the Long Barrows as a circular burial mound, that rose ever higher towards the sky.

Figure 46 *Bronze Mirror from Birdlip, Gloucester.*

Another Bronze Mirror (Fig. 46) which had been found at a burial site at Birdlip, near Gloucester, has a similar pattern showing the seals as if swimming in the water. This flowing, curvilinear, symmetrical design is full of life and movement and once again confirms that the spiral interlacing artwork of the Gael can be traced back to the gyrating movements of the seal as it swims in the sea, cavorting here and there at play. To compare the circular head, eyes and snout of the seals shown on the back of the mirrors, turn back to Figure 6 and observe the exceptionally close resemblance of the Inquisitive Seal to those seals illustrated on the mirrors.

It is interesting to reflect on the origin of the overall shape of the hand-mirror. Lloyd and Jenny Laing mention in their book *The Picts and the Scots*, page 110, 'A recent study of Roman mirrors has suggested that the models for Pictish mirror symbols should be sought in the Roman world'! This suggestion I consider misleading!

I believe that the hand-mirror owes its shape and design to a stone circle, and the handle images the avenue leading from the circle to a smaller satellite cairn. Not only was the hand-mirror used to reflect one's image, but it also held the religious significance of the belief in life after death, possibly reflecting the spirit of the deceased.

Incidentally, the Picts and the Irish at that time despised everything with a Roman connection. Scholars sometimes appear to ignore that Britain and Ireland had their own civilisation long before the arrival of the pagan Romans.

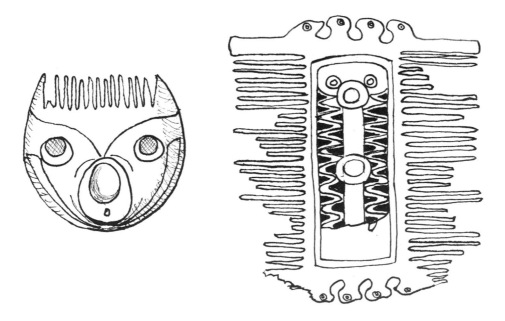

Figure 47 *Bone hand-combs.*

The mirror and comb can be found inscribed on many of Scotland's standing symbol stones. The comb, representing cleanliness, indicates another cairn positioned close to the main circle or mirror, where the deceased may have been placed possibly on a raised platform to enable the flesh to be picked clean by the fowl of the air. The body was then purified prior to it being interred or cremated.

Two examples of early hand-combs are shown in Figure 47, the smaller rounded comb from a crannog at Langbank, on the River Clyde. The decorative rounded face and eyes are those of a seal. The larger comb came from Dunadd, in Argyllshire. The central design of this comb is portraying the passageway of a tomb, with its stalls or cells indicated by the saw-tooth triangular pattern. From this design the eyebrow pattern developed, becoming the 'omega' symbol for the End. The design at the head of the passage tomb illustrated on the comb relates to the seal. The carved decoration appearing at either end of the comb is also depicting seals' heads.

The importance of the seal has been shown with the portal dolmens being held aloft by the stone seal orthostats. Portal dolmens may have eventually been considered as a warning to incoming farmers. This may be witnessed by the host country's determination to illustrate ownership of the land by marking territorial boundaries, combined with informing the farmers of their own religious belief. The coastal people as sea-faring traders may have retraced the steps of the incoming farmers by building dolmen structures on the trading routes used by the farmers throughout Europe, the Mediterranean, and on into the land of Canaan, whence they believed the farmers had earlier come.

Many academics inform us that it was the Romans who by introducing Latin and Greek brought civilisation to the so-called savages of Western Europe. The Romans looked on the Greeks as having created a new modern society, which they in turn further developed; yet, looking back on the Greeks, archaeological evidence sheds some light on their religious practices. No buildings have been found on the Greek mainland that can be said with certainty to have been built for sacred purposes during the Aegean Early Bronze Age, c.2800–1900BC, whereas in Britain and Ireland sacred megalithic structures date back to c.7600BC. Many seemingly Greek myths and legends may originate from our own islands.

CHAPTER 5
The Arrival of Farming

*F*arming, as a commercial enterprise, commenced as early as 10,000 BC in Asia Minor from where it slowly spread to other regions and nations. These farmers were themselves nomadic, continually searching for fresh green pastures and water for their ever-expanding herds. This was a very important time for these early people as they were creating the basic foundation of a new market economy, on which the nations of the world would eventually depend for their wealth and power, an economy to rival the existing mining and stone industries.

The first groups of farmers may have spoken an early form of Indo-European language similar to that spoken by the Gaels. The ladies of the Hebridean Islands sing a chant which is identical to the chant of Ethiopian women. Despite the difference in both language and race, it would appear that the origin of this chant may well have been taken by the early seafarers from Western Europe to Ethiopia.

Ladies in the Hebridean Isles are renowned for singing as they work together as a team, sitting on either side of a long table to hand wash the tweed cloth fresh from the weaving looms. The new woven cloth is washed and placed on the table where it is pounded by hand, rolled and kneaded, as the women lift, then slap the material down on the table passing it from one to the other, while they sing in Gaelic with an appropriate rhythmical beat. I wonder if these ladies give any thought to the sheep which had arrived on these islands 6000 years ago resulting in the successful breeding of animals that supply the wool for the Harris Tweed industry of today.

Megalithic dolmens and menhirs had been built in Brittany about 6000BC, whereas farming methods had spread to north-western France shortly after 5000BC. Settlements were to follow on the Channel Islands, established by farming communities, who around the same time crossed over to Britain's west coast.

This was a new economy being founded by the farmers, based on a matriarchal society, reaching Britain by 4500BC, and Ireland by 4000BC, although some of the oldest known megalithic tombs at Carrowmore, in Ireland, were built about 4800BC. Farming groups are said to have moved north to reach the Orkney Islands by c.3500BC. These dates of the incoming farmers are important and may be linked to some of the later megalithic monuments, built by the indigenous coastal people. This enables us to understand the events that led up to a possible turbulent integration that may have taken place with the arrival of farming groups, as they attempted to co-exist with the peoples of Western Europe. It may well be that some nomadic farmers reaching Western Europe found that the native Europeans had already commenced farming, and were themselves looking for land for further grazing and expansion.

By c.4000BC the coastal and seafaring traders in Canaan had erected dolmens on the Golan Heights in an attempt to assert that they too had justifiable claims to the land, indicating that the land was not there just for the benefit of nomadic farmers, but belonged to the indigenous people of that country.

It is interesting that the Mesolithic people in Europe may have considered that it was from the Eastern Mediterranean that the early farmers had originated, as indicated by the assembly of their megalithic structures in Canaan. At Telgezer, in the land of Canaan, they also made an alignment of white standing stones to form an avenue, which along with the dolmens can still be seen today in Palestine. This led me to look back to the Old Testament where we read of the migration of Abram from Chaldea to Canaan :

'And Terah took Abram his son, Lot the son of Haran his son's son, and Sarai his daughter-in-law, his son Abram's wife; and they went forth with them from Ur of the Chaldees, to go into the land of Canaan; and they came unto Haran, and dwelt there.'

The family remained at Haran, until the death of Tera.

In these few words the scriptures record the first act in the drama of a nation's birth. It was in Egypt that Abram acquired his main wealth of sheep, cattle, donkeys, camels, and male and female slaves. With his family, possessions, and his herds, Abram was able to build up a tribe which included his retainers, and they prospered and expanded to become a powerful nation.

At first the matriarchal farming groups were accepted by the host countries, however this welcome may have turned later to open hostility, which may have continued for many thousands of years as farmers became more powerful claiming more land and making further progress, resulting in them becoming the aristocrats in this new world. This land-grabbing by the farmers may have been strongly opposed by the indigenous Mesolithic people, who, as seafarers and coastal dwellers, may have retaliated by building more portal dolmen tombs to prove their rights to the land and to indicate and promote their own religious beliefs.

Social upheavals may have commenced in the late centuries of the fourth millennium BC, leading to open enmity throughout Europe between the incoming nomadic farmers, the coastal dwellers, and the seafarers, continuing right up to the time when the Pretannic people accepted Christianity.

The Western European way of life had already been established on a religious megalithic stone and mineral economy, which had necessitated the earlier introduction of their own indigenous farming community in order to feed an ever-growing religious seal-stone oriented population.

To the farmers the symbol of the sheep's horns referred to the matriarchal control held by the ladies of the farming groups in Europe and possibly also in some of the eastern Mediterranean countries. The spiral of the sheep's head can be found inscribed on some of Scotland's symbol stones. One of these symbols, mistakenly described as a tuning fork, relates to the farming communities' stalled chamber tombs, and others to some of their long barrows, as shown by the following symbols:

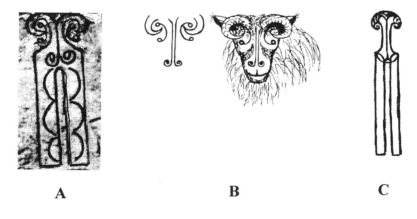

A   B   C

Figure 48

Stone Age Alpha

Fig. 48A

This hieroglyphic symbol appears on the Abernethy Class I Symbol Stone, found positioned at the bottom of the Round Tower outside the entrance to St. Bride's Parish Church in Abernethy, Perthshire. The symbol comprises the spiral head of a sheep, not a ram, and is positioned at the top of the geometric design of a plan view of a stalled-chamber tomb.

The central passageway of this geometric configuration is the corridor that leads to the stalls or cells situated on either side of the passageway. These stalls are indicated and highlighted by the arc type symbol known as an eyebrow symbol. These eyebrow motifs have both continental and Aegean affinities and may represent one of the earliest symbols used for the last letter in the Greek alphabet, 'omega', the 'End', which is rather appropriate as the cell or the stall within the chamber is the last resting place for the departed. This same eyebrow symbol appears on the decorated funerary chalk drums which had been buried in a grave at Folkton Wold, Humberside, is also found on stone monuments, and on the stone work above the entrance to St. Serf's Church, Dunning, Perthshire. This church and its burial grounds are enclosed by a cashel, the eyebrow symbol referring to those interred within its grounds.

The plan view of the Knowe of Yarso Chambered Tomb, Rousay, Orkney, approximate length 47 feet, is strikingly similar to the smaller scaled geometric plan view depicted on the Abernethy Class I Stone.

Fig. 48B

The artistic, spiral design of the horns of a sheep illustrate the continuing design of the scroll of the spiral of life and its link with the power held and wielded by the ladies of the farming communities arriving in Britain and Ireland. Early people were well aware of the authority displayed by the scroll head of the sheep located at the top of these symbolic designs also shown on Figures 48A and C. This was the emblem of a woman's supreme power in a tribal society.

Fig. 48C

Once again the symbolic figure of the sheep's head is located at the head of this geometric plan view of a long barrow, with its long central corridor. Many, many stalls or cells were placed on either side of the passageway, which can be well over 100 feet in length, hence the reason the eyebrow symbol is not shown on this smaller scaled plan view.

The sheep's horns are included in many forms of artwork, referred to today as Celtic Art! Artwork had been established in Western Europe long before 5500 BC, but this may have been a further development by the incoming farmers in Britain and Ireland around 4500 BC. This scroll-type of artwork became integrated with the basic skills of the talented megalithic artists in Britain and Ireland, who had their own spiral figures relating to the seal mammal, which they had inscribed on stone and boulders long, long before the arrival of the Celts to Britain in c.500 BC. The coming of the Celts with their iron-working skills would have been accepted by the artistic, indigenous people of Britain and Ireland as a further extension of their creative art to promote their own existing culture.

Long before the arrival of the Celts, people moved freely back and forth from Gaul, as miners and geologists in search of new supplies of lead, copper, silver and gold. They integrated with the coastal people and accepted their customs and beliefs in sea-creatures leaping from the water in an attempt to unite with their sky-gods. These new arrivals populated south-west England, the west coast of Scotland, and Ireland.

Farming, however, had come to stay and did much to influence the way of life in Western Europe. Farmers no longer required to be nomadic. They had observed that the indigenous people had already established settlements, including resting-places for their revered dead, who had been returned to the 'beginning of life' i.e., as they saw it, to the mother seal. The farmers also built their own burial chambers where they highlighted the sheep as one of the main providers of the wealth and power for a tribe. The long barrows built by the farmers had cells set up on either side of the passageway which may have been used as stalls for protecting their breeding stock during harsh winter periods.

The writer recalls as a child being evacuated after the blitz in 1941 from Greenock to Laurencekirk, in Kincardineshire, and vividly remembers visiting an aunt in Cove, outside Aberdeen. Here the old lady and her son lived in a rectangular, thatched cottage overlooking the North Sea from high and dangerous cliffs. To gain access to the house it was necessary to enter through the passageway of the stalled byre to reach the front door. This, I gather, had been the accepted custom for many crofters.

Kirkmadrine Christianised Stone

The Kirkmadrine Christian Stone, from the Rhinns of Galloway, a classic example of the homage paid by ancient man to the seal, had at one time been the central seal stone placed within a small satellite ceremonial circle, functioning in conjunction with a much larger stone circle. This pagan pillar-stone had been Christianised and rededicated thousands of years later by clerics claiming the Chi-Rho symbol as a Christian emblem.

Figure 49 *Kirkmadrine Stone.*

The triangular-shaped head of this stone is the head of a seal, and is similar to some of the orthostats sculptured to support the capstone of a dolmen; it may also have been a form of overseer positioned within its own cairn to witness the ceremonies taking place within a stone circle. The circle shown encompassing the cross may also have been the symbol of the wheel-type sun-god; it may have indicated a sacred round barrow located within the Rhinns, which had earlier been the tribe's ancestral tomb and ceremonial place of worship, witnessed by the hooked crosier of the high priest.

The Greek letter 'A' has been added to represent the beginning of their conversion to Christianity. The early clerics were well aware of the meaning of 'alpha', and that the Christian converts related this symbol to the old megalithic 'V', which to them meant the beginning of life on earth.

The Kirkmadrine Stone is similar to the central stone found within the small satellite circle adjacent to the Ring of Brodgar, in Orkney (Fig.50). This large ring forms a perfect circle of 340 feet in diameter, which is exactly 125 megalithic yards – a megalithic yard being the standard prehistoric unit of measurement of length equalling 2.75 feet, as established by Professor Thom.

Figure 50 *Ceremonial Pillar Stone, Orkney.*

This central pillar stone with its images of seals is from the Brodgar satellite circle, and closely resembles the overall shape of the Kirkmadrine Stone. If the reader can imagine looking down upon the larger ring of the Brodgar stones and consider an avenue leading to its smaller satellite circle, it is then easy to associate the larger circle combined with the smaller circle as the outline of a mirror. These early people looked upon their circle as a mirror reflecting their belief in a form of worship to the firmament.

Orkney has a vast range of exciting prehistoric monuments, which provide unrivalled insight into how early people lived. The village of Skara Brae was constantly inhabited for most of 600 years, from 3100- 2500BC. The homes were built of local dry stone, the internal fittings included stone built dressers with cupboards, and stone slabs formed a box bed for a sleeping area; sewers located under each house were also built of stone. In the centre of each house is a kerbed central hearth, with a number of recumbent 'seal' seating stones scattered around; frontal designs of the seals' head are also faintly visible, forming part of the stone decorative fixtures, as shown in Figure 51.

Figure 51 *Ancient home at Skara Brae, Orkney.*

Life in Western Europe was steadfastly coupled to the inclusion of sea-creatures in a form of sacred worship, which grew apace with the simplification of the portal dolmens leading towards the construction of round barrows and circles. People had other religious reasons for building circular structures, as they believed that more than one large symbolic stone was required to oversee the ceremonies and witness the ritual transfer of the spirit taking place; hence the formation of a circular ring of pillar stones to contain the dynamic belief of the origin of man and the need to keep evil forces at bay during the transfer of the spirit of the deceased from within the confines of the circle. Around the same period that Skara Brae had been inhabited, the people on the Island of Lewis were also active in creating a settlement, leading to the erection between 2900 and 2600BC of the intriguing cross-like formation of the Callanish Standing Stones.

Further south in the Irish Sea, sandwiched between Britain and Ireland, is the Isle of Man, a well-known independent island with its own government and laws. The island is host to the largest circle yet found in our immediate vicinity. This circle, stated by Professor Timothy Darvill to be around 500m in diameter, almost one third of a mile, is of a remarkable size, covering a wide area. Within the circle further evidence was also discovered of the presence of a Mesolithic site which had a ceremonial stone placed within a pit or well. This stone I recognised as having been sculptured as a seal's head.

CHAPTER 6
Lakeland's Circular Monuments

One of the earliest stone circles to have been found in Britain may have been built in the English Lake District in Cumbria around 3200BC. In what I believe may have been a highly populated area, the quarrying of stone and its by-products were the main activity for the people. These early people may also have further sculptured the naturally-shaped hills shown in the background of Figure 52. This stone culture can be viewed at the fascinating Castlerigg Stone Circle, Keswick.

Note the 'V' on the folds of the clerics robes in relation to the 'V' on the stone, and how his head appears from the 'V' of his collar. His mitre also indicates a definite 'V' shape. All refer to the beginning.

Figure 52 *Right-hand entrance stone.*

This is one of the most interesting and revealing stone circles built in the Lake District. This spacious open air theatre, itself encircled by a panoramic background of sculptured hills and fells, overlooks a raised plateau surmounted by a ring of shapely monolithic pillars, that appear to stretch ever upwards to reach the skies. Here in this setting of breathtaking beauty, one absorbs the intense feeling of changing grandeur of this unfolding vista. This grandiose scene creates mystique and wonder, as one attempts to grasp and indeed unravel the skills of our ancient forebears, who indubitably had a strong belief in nature linked hand in hand with their unswerving faith in God.

The entrance to the circle is flanked by two upright stones, where the right hand stone is inscribed with several 'V' shapes, appearing near the top (Fig.52) indicating the 'beginning' of life for a sea-creature. This stone shows an inscribed head of a seal looking down with its snout to the ground. Invert the photograph and find other seals with their heads positioned as if resting on the ground. Note the small boulder on the left of the inverted photograph also indicates a seal's head on the ground. Return the photograph to its true position and look carefully at the other entrance stone; now turn the photograph clockwise on its side, and observe the head of a seal looking skywards.

The recumbent stone, facing due east, reveals the feature of a sculptured open type mouth positioned towards the south (Fig. 53). This stone is located beside the stone sanctuary, also facing east. Note the lozenge pattern.

Figure 53 *Recumbent stone.*
By kind permission of G.E.Peterson

The open 'V' shaped type mouth portrays a number of sea-creatures emerging, one of which is another seal with its mouth open appearing from the upper part of the seal's tail. To the right of the recumbent stone are two upright stones (not shown), the nearest of which is representing a seal's head looking upwards facing the recumbent stone; while the other stone is also a head of a seal facing north but looking upwards. Behind these stones lie the sanctuary, attached to the east-facing stones. The stone in the sanctuary on the right is a seal, as if its mouth were wide open facing eastwards ready to catch the first glimmer of light from the rising sun. This sanctuary may have been the enclosure for the dead, whose spirit, it was believed, would rise with the rising sun to be transferred as a seal to the heavens.

It is now a known fact that pregnant seals move to the eastern end of an island and give birth as the sun rises in the east.

The stone with its seal image, shown in Figure 54, is unnaturally hemmed in by plastic tape, the concept of the seal at first appearing as if it were stretching to peer over the strange plastic tape within which it has found itself confined. Another stone seal figure with the characteristic triangle clearly defined around its eye is positioned to the right. (The plastic tape was a temporary barrier while grass and turf were renewed!)

Figure 54 'To the hills I lift my eyes'.

Stone circles were a development from the court tombs and the round barrows, when it was decided to have a ring of stones to assist the single overseer stone. The main purpose of erecting these circular stone monuments had been to harness and focus the rays of light to enable the smooth transfer of the dead to a new life and a new beginning. In an attempt to have control of the ceremony, and to deter evil forces from influencing the event, a series of stones was erected to form a circle, each stone becoming a witness or an overseer, guiding and supporting the spirit of the departed. This can be witnessed very clearly at Castlerigg, as sculptured stones look to the east, while others face the west, the north, and the south as sentinels, watching and guarding over the spirit of the dead, as it rose with the rising sun.

The author has always lived in an area surrounded by hills and overlooking a river. This may possibly have influenced, and assisted, my understanding of the traditions of early people, who also had selected areas of scenic beauty in which not only to build their homes but also to erect sacred burial chambers.

While studying the sculptured seals in the Castlerigg Circle, I recalled the haunting melody of a song, heard in a church in the Strathearn valley, located between the Ochil Hills and the Grampian Mountains. The words of this song would have been openly welcomed and clearly understood by the Mesolithic and Neolithic people.

To the Hills

To the hills I lift my eyes, The distant hills before me;
Hills that rise to reach the skies, and spread their glory o'er me.
Planted by omnipotent hand, By divine appointment they stand;
To the hills I lift my eyes, The beck'ning hills before me.

Eyes may scan the dizzy height, And human feet stand on it;
Only faith, in mystic flight, Can see the realms beyond it.
Steeper than the mountains of time, Higher than the loftiest climb,
O'er the hills I lift my eyes; From hence my help is coming.

To the hills I'll turn again, Away from earthly slumber,
There to gain the topmost plain; May naught my way encumber.
On the highest summit I'll stand; There to view the long-promised land,
Though my eyes look to the skies, I lift my heart to heaven.

Tune - **Ochills**   By **Ernest Rance**

These words, based on Psalm 121, 'I to the hills will lift mine eyes,' would have been inspirational to the basic religious beliefs and understanding of these early people and indeed are significant to Christians to-day. One can envisage the acceptance of such words spoken by the early clerics, who came to preach to them within their learning centres of circular and lozenged enclosures and on hilltop retreats. This Western European civilisation at a later date caused great concern to the authorities in Rome, who saw the people of Britain and Europe as a force which, if merged with the people of the Mediterranean, could destabilise their far-flung Empire.

There are many carved seal heads in the ring of stones at Castlerigg, a magnificently positioned ring, comprising forty-two stones, located on a plateau above Keswick, and overlooked by the Skiddaw brood of hills which include the third highest peak in the Lake District. On examining the photograph (Fig.54) there would appear to be a circle and shapes of seals'

heads depicted near the top of the hill in the background! This may indicate an earlier or a ceremonial site, and may be another reason for the location of the Castlerigg Stone Circle with its fascinating amphitheatre.

Another fine example from the Castlerigg Stone Circle is highlighted by the shadows forming the main features of a seal's eye and head, along with a faint lozenged pattern as illustrated in Figure 55.

Figure 55 *'Though My Eyes Look to the Skies'.*

One other interesting Castlerigg stone with its triangular construction lines still visible depicts the seal's head again looking steadfastly upwards (Fig. 56). On the bottom left hand corner, outwith the triangular construction line, is yet another figure of a seal facing downwards. At the right hand corner another large head is portrayed. With the portrayal of seals at each corner of this monolith it is quite obvious that early man had an unswerving faith in the regeneration of the deceased, and in an afterlife.

Figure 56 '*There to View the Long-promised Land*'.

In south Cumbria, at Kirksanton, near Millom, located on the coastal plain with the mountains forming an interesting background, there are two standing stones known as The Giants' Graves (Fig. 57).

Figure 57 *'O'er the Hills I Lift My Eyes'.*

These two standing stones are all that is left of possibly a three-stone row or a true pair that had been erected in this area. It is quite apparent that many of the stones from this row have been dismantled in earlier years by farmers, as in the immediate vicinity at least eight stones have been built into the walls and used as gateposts. These standing stones clearly illustrate the seal as if paying homage to the heavens, especially the one in the background, where the sculptor had included ripples on the stone as if folds of skin at the back of the neck, as the seal stretches upwards to present another emerging seal.

The standing stone in the foreground has the head of a seal as if looking over to the other standing stone. This head is located at the left hand side formed by the obtuse angle, within which is an acute angle forming the snout of the seal. This head appears to emerge from the 'V' shape gouged out on this stone, as if representing the birth of another seal from the flippered tail ponting heavenwards. These people were past masters at inscribing double images on stones and boulders, as they obtained their skills by carefully studying the unique camouflaged body of the seal, which portrays one of the finest examples of camouflage to be found in the animal kingdom.

King Arthur's Round Table

In nearby Penrith, in the Parish of Yanwath, there are several henges, two of which are relatively close together, the approximate distance from centre to centre being about 500 yards. The sketch shows them at half this distance.

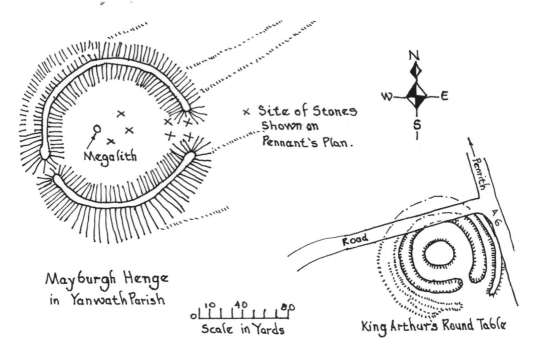

x Site of Stones
Shown on
Pennant's Plan.

Megalith

Mayburgh Henge
in Yanwath Parish

Scale in Yards

King Arthur's Round Table

Road

Figure 58 Mayburgh Henge and King Arthur's Table.

King Arthur's Round Table is only 400 yards from Eamont Bridge, occupying a site partly cut into by the road. This henge is different from its near neighbour Mayburgh Henge, as it has a small ditch which had at one time encircled its outer diameter of around 60 yards. It had been recorded by Stukeley that the Scots Army accompanying Charles II to Worcester camped on this site. (Stukeley, Itinerarium Curiosum II.)

The Mayburgh Henge is ¼ mile south-west of Eamont Bridge, and is positioned on a small knoll. It consists of a rampart varying in height from 8–15 ft. and encloses a flat area of about 1½ acres. According to *Pennant's Tour in Scotland*, in the 18th century there had been eight stones; three had been clustered with the existing one, and four grouped flanking the main entrance. A small modern gap is located on the S.W.

The main entrance faces directly due east, allowing the first light of day to filter its rays between the trees, where at one time there had been upright pillars forming the entrance; the light from the sun converged directly on the 9 feet tall standing-stone of the seal, illuminating it as it stood proudly in the centre of the henge, heralding a new beginning to the day. Entrances to henges and stone circles, and the opening of the Torc neck bands are closely related to one another, as the openings also represented the passageway of life from birth through adulthood to death and finally regeneration, which represented a new beginning.

The placing of a body on an overhead structure held upright by vertical wooden tree trunks had been part of a ceremony performed by the indigenous people of America. On the death of a warrior the North American Indians, as part of their ritual, attempted to assist the spirit of their departed brave to pass from this life into the happy hunting-grounds. The burial grounds of the American Indian can be linked to our stone circles and henges, where the people who built our megalithic tombs were also attempting to assist a smooth passage for the deceased from this life to a new life above.

Figure 59 *North American Indian Moon Spider Crosses.*

It is interesting to find that the North American Indians' burial grounds had a formation similar to our henges, as shown by these sketches of their enclosures highlighting the spider cross. When considering our circular barrows and the round bases of some of our Neolithic funerary vases, one can find the cross symbol included as part of the inherent design, directly related to the sun cross. Let us ponder here as the North American Indians' cross divides the circle of the spider into four equal segments, which could equally well represent Mayburgh's four centrally positioned stones. Furthermore the entrance into the North American circle illustrates two small circles, similar in conception to the entrance of stone pillars at Mayburgh Henge.

The spider as illustrated is similar to the giant ground spider of the Nazca desert in Southern Peru, where the strange shape of some ancient Nasca skulls has fuelled speculation about extraterrestrials. What is interesting about this area is the Nascas' association with large trapezoids pointing to the mountain gods. Orca, the killer whale, was one of their gods, with the spiral eye of the whale featuring prominently within their design. Another whale carried a trophy of a severed head as an offering for the mountain gods, who provided the water in this drought-ridden land.

Wigwams are normally the homes one envisages for the North American Indian, yet the Indians such as the Pawnee and Omaha from the Missouri River area lived in semi-permanent villages of dome-shaped, earth-covered lodges. These lodges were similar to the circular earth houses used by ancient people living in Western Europe. The Tlingit tribe of Northwest Canada, who live in the coastal area around Skagway, carve wooden figures of salmon metamorphosing into humans (Fig. 60). This is similar to the thinking of early people of Western Europe who had believed that humans had evolved from the seal. Figure 130 portrays a human head emerging from the Riskbuie stone.

It is taken for granted that the interesting spiral curvilinear designs are credited to the Celt, yet in the Southwest of America in Arizona, around 200BC, a group of committed farmers, known as the prehistoric Hohokam, made spiral designs similar to those attributed to the Celts and illustrated by the Spiral Hohokam bowl (Fig. 60).

Figure 60 *Indian art work.*

Some of the finest pre-Celtic spirals found inscribed on boulder rock can be traced to Scotland and to Newgrange in Ireland.

Newgrange

In Britain and Ireland there are a number of passage-graves ranking among the finest in Western Europe; these include the exceptionally well-built stone chamber of Maes Howe, Orkney, and the remarkable construction of Newgrange, in Co. Meath, Ireland.

Figure 61 *Newgrange Passage Grave.*
By kind permission of Mrs Claire O'Kelly.

The stones placed before the entrance to Newgrange are indeed spectacular. The central stone is emphasising the camouflaged patterns which early man had observed on the body of the spotted harbour seal. The head of the seal on this stone is on the left hand side, and the 'V' flippered tail on the right. Note how the recumbent seal stone on the right forms the basis of the saltire, nosing up in greeting, as it were, to the tail of the central decorated seal stone. On the front of the left hand stone are seals swimming in the sculptured rippled water, with the faintly sculptured 'V' of its tail presented to the central decorated stone. K.McNally, in his book *Standing Stones and other monuments of early Ireland*, refers to Newgrange, as: **'The most penetrating excavation work ever undertaken at any prehistoric site in Ireland so far has revealed much about its construction and purpose; but other secrets, such as the cryptic symbolism of its beautiful decorated stones, remain inviolate.'** (*Standing Stones*, 1988, p.37)

Figure 62 *Chamber entrance and roof box during excavation.*

By kind permission of Mrs Claire O'Kelly.

The entrance to the passage with the Roof-box is indeed impressive, along with the intriguing decorative lozenge design. This diamond pattern design is directly attributed not only to the head of the seal but to its highly effective body camouflage. To fully appreciate the lozenge and triangular designs it is essential to understand the fundamental beliefs held by these people in their cult worship with the seal, coupled, as they saw it, to the origin of man. There is one other elemental recurring design depicted within these lozenge shapes, which is the formation of a natural Saltire emblem. In order to illustrate and prove these links it is necessary to study the photographs of seals, and attempt to comprehend the everyday way of life of Mesolithic man.

Figure 63 *Seal swimming on its side.*

The curved back of the seal when swimming on its side just below the surface of the water helps to highlight the triangular shape of its head, and the general overall shape of the seal can be related to orthostats. It also clarifies the well-formed rounded curve of its back which can be affiliated to the symbol of a crescent appearing on standing stones and as the integral design of the seal on jewellery, which will be discussed shortly. This triangular shape of the head is one of the main features appearing on ancient stone monuments, which continued as a design, even today in Scotland as a company logo. Another three-sided shape appears just around the eye of the seal, with the eye positioned centrally encompassed by the fascinating natural features of a triangular design that is part of the integral body camouflage of the seal.

Figure 64 *Triangle appearing around the eye.*

Figure 64 shows this triangular boss-shape appearing around the eye of the seal, and a further speckled lozenge shape in the centre positioned at the base of the neck, observed as the mammal leaves the water. The near straight line appears in the area just above the seal's eye as if it were an eyebrow; emanating from this line are two slightly curved skin or bone projections which then come together to form the apex of this triangular shape terminating below the eye.

As the seal watched me, I observed further triangular patterns on its body, similar to the patterns appearing on megalithic structures, and on funerary urns (Fig.65). This was quite remarkable, and upon examining my colour photograph more carefully (Colour Plate No.4) I observed that the body shape and colouring of the seal are in fact an intriguing camouflage design which acts as a deterrent to its predators. These designs portray patterns of several heads of seals, both small and large, and further triangular eyebrow patterns forming around its body. My next observation took me totally by surprise as the side flippers at certain instances of movement can reveal the shape of the seal's head on its body, where a head looks forward and another looks to its tail. There is no doubt that these early people had an in-depth knowledge of the coastal seals and their environment.

During their burial ceremonies the symbolic seal features and designs were incorporated by the megalithic people to convey their respect and farewell to their revered departed. This esteem for the dead, in conjunction with their seal-cult beliefs, had been an integral part of their normal caring way of life, attested not only on stone, but also incorporated on their jewellery and the decorative designs appearing on funerary urns and flint implements.

Figure 65 *Funerary urns.*

The triangular and lozenge designs appear on three funerary vessels, as sketched in Figure 65. The largest of the three crematory urns is held in the National Museum, Dublin. This encrusted vessel has a triangular design complete with a smaller circle, representing the eye and the head of the seal, and is seen as a form of camouflage on the body of the seal. The small triangles in the lower second tier indicate seal heads appearing in a light sea.

The seal emerges from the lozenge in the third tier as the ancestral spirit of the dead, reaching upwards to the skies. The endowed spirit of the seal emerging is also highlighted by some of the so-called blocking stones, placed as if at the entrance to a chambered tomb to indicate the spiritual rising of the dead (Colour Plate No.12).

The smaller urn on the right comes from Rudston, west of Bridlington, Yorkshire. Here within the triangular pattern at the bottom of this urn there is the small circle imaging the seal's eye. The dotted pattern indicates pebbles on the beach and those irregular zigzag designs above are showing a stormy sea, followed nearer the top with a series of horizontal lines indicating the calmer water of the foreshore with a line of cliffs shown by the triangular design rising in the background. This same design can be observed on some of the impressive buildings in Portugal.

The small urn is one of three chalk drums found buried with a five year old child, at Folkton, North Yorkshire. The eyebrow symbol of a seal is announcing the early symbol of 'omega', the end. The small diamond symbol is depicting the mouth of the seal and also indicates the last resting place. The two 'V' designs are lying on their sides representing the ancient 'A'- the beginning. These two ancient symbols of 'A' also relate to the saltire design signifying a welcome to the next phase of the child's life after death; these symbols also relate to the head of the seal and its whiskers, indicating the last resting place for the child, and the beginning of a new life after death. These ancient symbols of 'A' have been been divided symmetrically and positioned horizontally with a small pattern of diamond shapes indicating water from which both seal and man had evolved. This is a similar message to that confirmed by the roof-box lozenge design sculptured at the very entrance to the passageway at Newgrange, and by the recumbent stones encircling Newgrange, forming the saltire design of a greeting of welcome to the deceased.

The decorative roof-box at Newgrange has other sculptured heads of seals appearing at either end of the lintel. These sculptured heads also appear on the ends of Passage Roofslabs 1 and 2. Passage Roofslab 1 is located directly below the decorated lozenge designed lintel, whereas Passage Roofslab 2 is the capstone shown in the foreground, supported by two orthostats which provide the entrance to the passageway and to the inner chamber. The roof-box is exciting as Passage Roofslab 1 has the inverted design of a sculptured seal on its underside as if lying stretched out in an upside-down position, similar to the seal shown in Figure 14. Just below this inverted seal and positioned near the centre of the box is

yet another figure of a seal lying in the normal way. This is not the first time the author has come across an inverted seal; the upturned capstone lying beside the footpath near Pentre Ifan (Fig.15) also illustrates this feature.

As the sun-light shone through the Roof-box, the light shone on both sculptured seals, which cast their shadows on the upper orthostats in the passageway. The High Priest at Newgrange may have interpreted the inverted seal as either ascending or descending from the skies to meet the reincarnated spirit, now embodied in the smaller seal, to convey or accompany the souls of the departed to begin a new life.

Figure 66 *The Sun's rays pass through the entrance and the roof-box.*
By kind permission of the Office of Public Works, Ireland

During the sunrise on December 21,1969, it was established by Professor O'Kelly: 'At exactly 9.45am (BST) the top edge of the ball of the sun appeared above the local horizon and at 9.58 am the first pencil of direct sunlight shone through the roof-box and right along the passage to reach the tomb chamber floor as far as the front edge of the basin stone in the end chamber.' (*Newgrange, 1996*, page 29, by Claire O'Kelly)

Figure 67 *View looking towards entrance.*
By kind permission of the Office of Public Works, Ireland

Figure 67 is a view from the passageway looking towards the entrance, and highlights the interesting pattern, carved on the orthostat, of three spirals representing the two eyes and the snout of the seal; other orthostats and corbelled stones in the passageway also portray the sculptured head of the seal. Above the spiral motif are inscribed lozenge shapes ascribing to the final resting place of the dead.

At one time a ring of standing stones encircled this mound referred to as 'The Great Circle', which is approximately 340 ft in diameter. It is thought that there had once been 35 stones forming this circle.

Figure 68 *Symbol Stones form part of The Great Circle.*
By kind permission of Mrs Claire O'Kelly

Scholars have recorded that there are no symbols appearing on any of the stones forming part of the Great Circle; this is certainly not the case, as early people would never have erected a stone unless it bore some symbolic significance to their early beliefs. Four of the Great Circle stones positioned opposite the entrance are sculptured stones with inscribed symbols relating to the seal and the whale. The stone in the background is attesting to the upright seal stretching upwards to the skies. This stone has also a diamond pattern located in the centre with its apex about to penetrate the shadow. Within this lozenge shape is the seal's head and snout pointing downwards, with other seal features also shown on this stone.

The next upright stone to the right confirms that these early people believed that the whale had created the seal. This stone is said to have a fault, but this would have been noted by the sculptors who had depicted an open type mouth of a sea-creature, and a seal emerging from this 'V' shaped aperture. The eye of the seal can readily be determined to the right on the rounded shape of the stone; other seals are also observed. Appearing on the third stone from the left is another interesting crescent-shaped symbol of the seal with its head, snout and eye clearly visible at the top of the stone, the shadow possibly indicating an open mouth. A large lozenge shape in the centre of the stone is imaging the eye of a large seal taking in the entire shape of the stone. Again there are other seals shown on this stone, and on the one in the foreground.

CHAPTER 7

Seals on Bronze and Stone

One book under the heading of National Museum of Ireland, entitled *Early Celtic Art in Ireland*, by Eamonn P. Kelly, describes on page 39 Ireland's Monasterevin bronze discs as follows: 'The curvilinear decoration of the disc *may* be a stylised representation of a human face.'

Bronze discs

The decorated Bronze discs from Monasterevin, Co. Kildare, are indeed of interest but it is not a stylised human face; shown within the metal spun disc is the sea-cult design of the rounded head, snout and eyes of a seal. Both discs have round eyes which represent the curvilinear shape of the seal. Note the overall similarity of this circular design with the aerial plan views of Avebury, Windmill Hill, and Stonehenge, and with the frontal view of the inquisitive seal (Fig. 6).

The outer circle of the bronze disc indicates the front view of the cylindrical body of a seal. The three quarter sized circle shows the head of the seal, the smaller swaged bead forming the circle located in the centre is its snout, with the lower spiral motif illustrating its mouth and whiskers. Above all the artist is emphasising the all-seeing curvilinear eyes of the seal. The snout depicts the ceremonial centre of a stone circle or a henge.

Figure 69 Bronze disc.

Another frontal view of a seal's head is illustrated in Figure 70, including a smaller outer circular body. The high quality of Irish metal work can be seen when examining the fragmentary bronze head-dress known as the 'Petrie Crown'. This fascinating object may be an early crown, belonging to one of the early Irish Neptune kings, who were reputed to be the rulers of the sea. The metal components may have been attached to the base of leather and cloth. The depicted design shown on this crown confirms the existence of the Neptune kings, and also the exalted position held by the seal in this society.

Figure 70 *Bronze disc.*

Figure 71 *Petrie's Bronze Crown.*

Colour Plate No.1 *Belas Knap.*

The mosaic artwork of the seal heads can be seen on the right hand side of the chamber. Note also the faint inscribed angles on the central recumbent seal-stone.

Colour Plate No.2 *Burren Wedge Tomb.*

Observe the large seal head on the innermost face of the right hand orthostat.

Colour Plate No. 3 *Men-Scryfa Symbol Stone.*
By kind permission of Peter Sentence

Early people when sculpturing these monolithic pillars attempted to portray several designs within a pattern, similar to the multi-emblems shown on the Indian Totem Pole. This appears to be a form of dual thinking and expression which can overlap the development of their beliefs. This pillar is such an example, as it can also portray the upright body of the seal with its flippered tail pointing to the sky in a 'V' shaped formation, creating the birth of a seal. The eye shown on the right hand side of the flipper is the false eye represented by the bulging knuckle that can be found on the flipper of the seal, as illustrated in Figure 8, Tapering Seal Body.

Colour Plate No. 4 *Camouflaged body.*

Between the head and the side flippers are two protruding triangular shapes that can also appear around the seal's eyes as eyebrows. Side flippers portray the dual head of a seal looking as if in two directions. At the top of the seal's back there are two large lozenge designs as an eyebrow and a circular eye. This configuration coupled to the side flippers takes on the frontal face of the seal.

Colour Plate No. 5 *'Le Dehus' Chamber, Guernsey.*
By kind permission of George Rankin

The lozenge pattern on the left hand pillar stone has an eye in the centre of the lower lozenge design depicting the head of the seal, looking towards the ground.

Colour Plate No.6 *West Kennet Long Barrow.*

By kind permission of the National Trust and English Heritage

Seal heads can be seen on the forecourt stones looking up and also looking down.

Colour Plate No.7 *Replica of a crescentic necklace.*

By kind permission of Kilmartin House Museum.

Note triangular shape of the head of the necklace and the sacred lozenge design appearing on it.

Colour Plate No. 8 *Recumbent Seal Stones at Newgrange.*

Seals greet one another with nose contact as do many animals, however the meeting of two seal heads form the saltire design of welcome, as indicated by the recumbent stones at Newgrange.

Colour Plate No. 9 *Prominent eyebrows of the seal.*

Note the triangular eyebrows and other camouflaged designs on the head and body of the seal that are also reflected on the water.

Colour Plate No.10
Large sculptured seal heads.

The heather in the foreground is a reasonable guide to the scale of these amazing sculptured Seal Heads.

The background landscape of boulders and rocks may also have been shaped by man to show the seal head. To confirm this one would require to examine these boulders and rocks on the hillside.

Details of smaller heads can be seen on Colour Plate No.11, at the right hand top of the lozenge carved boulder, especially the remarkable fine detail of the head observed on the far right. The seal head can also be seen on the protruding rock at the top right hand corner.

Colour Plate No.11
Smaller sculptured seal heads.

Colour Plate No.12 *Sculptured head of potential chamber.*

Positioned on the skyline is the entrance to a potential ancient unique chamber, with a large sculptured boulder of a seal head positioned at the front of the narrow entrance.

Colour Plate No. 13 *View of potential new chamber.*

A further interesting view of this large sculptured boulder clearly showing the head, eye, snout and curved cheek of the seal.

Colour Plate No. 14
St. John from the Book of Kells.

Colour Plate No. 15 *Tapered seal tail of Kilclooney Dolmen.*

The Petrie Crown symbolises the designs of two seals, which differ facially from one another, one seal shown on the left as if in deep solemn contemplation, whilst the other is shown smiling and knowingly displaying the wheel symbol of the sun-god. The conical coronet represents the tapering body shape of the seal, with its tail turned upwards pointing to and confirming that homage was paid to the sun. The sun/wheel cross is one of the oldest symbols known to man and can be traced from the Old World to the indigenous people of America.

The wheel cross also depicts a round barrow, the megalithic tomb associated with the origin of this particular tribe. It is intriguing to observe the presence of four different birds. These may have been intended as the grebe family which represented the flying transporter, similar to the goose and the merganser depicted on Scotland's symbol stones, that would carry the spirit of the departed to the skies above. The birds are migratory, and it is feasible that from a very early period early man, being inquisitive, may well have attempted to establish the destination of these birds by following their migratory journey.

Mesolithic people treated their dead with deep sincere respect. This high esteem manifests itself by their building of the megalithic dolmen tombs, which are distributed throughout Britain, Ireland, Sweden, Denmark, Germany, Belgium, France, Spain, Portugal, and on through the Mediterranean to Gamia in the Golan Heights and to the Galilee area. This indicates that the people of Western Europe had a direct influence on the people of the Middle East and their culture. Some of the symbols found on Scotland's symbol stones can be traced to symbols used by the Hittites, who may have moved from France to follow the European inland rivers to Greece, the Black Sea, and on to Turkey and Egypt at a later date.

Monolithic tombs and standing stones had played an important part in the lives of Western European societies, where they became one of the assembly points for the various tribes, to introduce laws, and to dispense the justice of their seal-culture. In making their laws they sealed an agreement in the presence of their sacred seal. This may be the origin of the meaning of " the seal of approval", or "the seal of authority", which was conveyed in the presence of these sacred monolithic seals! The Sarsen Stones supported a continuous ring of shaped lintels representing the mammal of the seal, thereby endorsing their seal of authority at the circle of Stonehenge. Later the seal of Dervorguilla de Balliol incorporated in the Statutes of Balliol College, Oxford, in 1282, is another example, to be discussed later in this book.

Some of our early inhabitants came from Spain, Gaul, and the Balkans. In Spain they refer to a stamp in Spanish as 'sello', which also means a seal, not the mammal which is known as 'foca'. In Greece the word for seal (the mammal) is 'phoca'. Phoca can be traced, in the myths and legends of the Greeks, to Phocus, the son of Aeacus, king of Aegina, whose mother was Psamathe who came from the Nereids, meaning wet people or sea-nymphs. Psamathe, in her attempt to thwart Aeacus' amorous embraces, turned herself back into a seal in order to escape his unwanted attention. Eventually she gave birth to Phocus, son of Aeacus. The Western European stories may be older than the Greek mythical versions, and may indicate the flow of our ancient western culture to the Mediterranean and beyond.

Prior to retiring to Perthshire, one of my hobbies had been sailing, and I recall on one occasion slipping 'Windward's' mooring, to sail up Loch Long, and on into Loch Goil, to lay anchor for the night opposite the ruin of Carrick Castle. At daybreak I was awakened by someone singing in German, then in Italian. On going up on deck I observed the singer with his back to me as he stood at the stern of a large motor vessel, his tenor voice re-echoing and reverberating from the close proximity of the purple-clad hills and mountains, hills that merged with the loch in the morning dawn as the singer's song travelled over the water into the bays and coves that formed a small natural fjord.

The singer was unaware that he had an admiring audience of seals, listening intently to his song. These seals may have been awakened from their upright sleeping position where their triangular snouts protruded above the becalmed water. Upon hearing the singer they had moved upwards out of the water to gaze with open inquisitive round black shining eyes of wonder, drawn by the voice of a talented impresario.

In the Moray Firth, the River Spey passes through the small town of Fochabers. Let us consider the link with the Iberian word for the seal as 'foca', and then link it with 'aber', meaning 'the head of.' This town's name may refer to the seal heads. Fochabers is well known for salmon, which, having escaped the many seals at the mouth or head of the River Spey, leap up-river to spawn. From Fochabers let us now cross the Moray Firth to the small town of Dingwall to investigate the Class I Stone in the local parish church.

Dingwall Parish Church Menhir

Figure 72 *Dingwall Class I Symbol Stone.*

    The churchyard of Dingwall is host to a Class I Symbol Stone, which may date back to at least the Bronze Age. The inscribed figure of a crescent had always been thought to be Pictish, and was considered by many people to represent the moon. After studying this crescent figure yet again, I now find that there are three seal heads, one at the left, another with its eye inscribed in the centre looking to the right, and the third is also looking to the right, above and to the right of the central seal's snout. Other seal heads can be observed on this stone.

Careful analysis of this stone reveals that the seal had been incised, complete with its flipper, and is positioned directly above another seal not so clearly defined. These seals depict the origin of the double crescent inscribed on other symbol stones indicating the merger that had taken place between two separate tribes.

The seal has been bisected by a broken arrow, which may have been added at a later date. This may have occurred when a Pictish tribe had earlier accepted Christianity. By breaking the arrow the Picts had illustrated their breaking away from their old tribal customs, and their acceptance of a new faith and a new way of life. Examining the apex of the broken arrow, it is noted that yet again the design of a small triangle is formed within the acute angle, and within the triangle itself is the head and the eye of the all-seeing seal. If on the other hand this broken arrow or 'V' symbol had been inscribed at an earlier date, it would have indicated the beginning of life after death.

The photograph shown earlier (Fig. 63) displays the lower seal swimming on its side, its head forming a triangle in which the eye of the seal is purposely placed. If the reader inverts this photograph and inclines it slightly downwards, the resemblance to the seal on the Dingwall stone is seen. The seal shown in Figure 63 is the shape and contour of the Pictish crescent which dates back to the Bronze Age and possibly even earlier. The head of the seal, complete with whiskers, takes on another profile as it swims on its side below the water; note how the shape of the head differs from the seal swimming above.

The shape of the head of this seal swimming in the orthodox way (*see* Fig.63) is similar to the two seals looking to the right within the crescent. The small bump on the head of the seal is a prominent feature sculptured and inscribed on many symbolic monoliths. The camouflaged design patterns appearing on the seal's body were understood by early man who copied these as sacred designs and recorded them on rocks, menhirs, and within their sacred burial chambers.

The tiny island of Gigha is only 6 miles long, and is positioned off the coast of the Mull of Kintyre. Mull of Kintyre was highlighted by Paul Macartney's famous song of the same name.

On the island of Gigha there are several interesting stones; two sites are to be found at opposite ends of the island. Referring back to the photograph of the seal (Fig. 64) the seal's head can be immediately related to the symbol stones found on this island.

The Tourist Board refer to these two stones as ancient mysteries from the past. The locals refer to them as The Druid Stone, and the other known in Gaelic as – Cnoc a'Bhodaich (Hill of the old man and the old woman).

'The Druid Stone' is located by the roadside to the north of the island. This stone is also referred to as The Hanging Stone.

THE ISLAND OF

Figure 73 Isle of Gigha.

Figure 74 *The Druid Stone.*
(Clach a' Thairbert)

The conventional local interpretation of this stone is that people found guilty at 'The Court Hill', located nearby, met their deaths on it. The photograph of the hanging stone portrays a sea-creature with its mouth open, as if it were ready to swallow its prey. One can clearly observe the eye of the sea-creature incised on this stone. An island court having found a person guilty of a heinous crime suspended the culprit by the neck between the formed open mouth of the stone until he/she expired. The mouth of this sea-creature has been carefully shaped to accept a person's head, without any hope of escape. To the right on the stone highlighted by shadow is an elongated seal head sculptured in relief.

The Hanging Stone of Gigha can be linked, in relation to shape, to the aerial plan view of the ancient Belas Knap Long Barrow, located in the Cotswolds, and to the miniscule symbol on Orkney (*see* Fig.122) and to metal ingots smelted and moulded in Cornwall. In the south-west of the island the two stones known as the 'Old Man and the Old Woman' can be found on top of a small mound.

Figure 75 *Cnoc a' Bhodaich.*
(The old man and the old woman)

These stones are located on the private land of Ardlamey farm, placed on the top of a small hillock, close to the west shore. The locals refer to the taller of the two stones as an old man wearing his cap, and the smaller as an old woman with a shawl around her shoulders! These figures placed on this small knoll dominate the landscape and the seascape, where the silhouette of the taller of the two stones portrays the form of a female seal, proudly sitting surveying the seas around her island domain. Making a closer inspection of the smaller and broader of the two stones, said to be the old hag, it revealed the shape and face of the heavier built bull-seal, not the old woman, but the old man. Both these stones may well go back to the Bronze Age.

Mr. MacNeill, the purser of the ferry boat, can trace his ancestors back in time to the Lord of the Isles. Upon our return to the mainland, our findings regarding the stones were made known to Mr.MacNeill, who was interested, as he confirmed that his father, and his father before him, believed that the seals around the coast held the spirits and the souls of their departed ancestors. This is a view held by many coastal and island dwellers in Britain.

Gigha is a small island, peaceful and relaxing, with fine scenic views especially enhanced as the sun sets over the distant hills and its dying rays illuminate the sea as seals lumber about at play on the foreshore.

The next stones to be visited are located at Inverurie, a town not on the coast but inland located between Fochabers and Aberdeen. Yet the seal is the dominant creature appearing on all three stones. The trio of Scotland's Class I Symbol Stones are positioned not far from the ruins of an old derelict church, overlooking small streams.

Scotland's Symbol Stones have been mentioned on several occasions, and for those readers who are not familiar with the current classification the three headings are briefly as follows:

Class III Symbol Stones are Pictish stone monuments depicting the cross in relief; the artwork is that of the descendants of the indigenous people. Normally they do not portray the animal and geometric symbols associated with the Picts.

Class II Symbol Stones are mainly of Pictish origin, with a Pictish cross and animal and geometric symbols illustrated in relief.

Class I Symbol Stones are pre-Christian, and said to be of undressed stone with animal and geometric symbols incised on them.

Most of these stones in my opinion have been carefully selected and sculptured to predetermined shapes, and then in many instances inscribed with animal, geometric and zoomorphic figures relating to their tribal origin.

It now appears that there are two schools of thought regarding the dating of the Class I stones. The majority of people believe them to be Pictish dating from around the 4th–5th century. Professor Charles Thomas, I understand, now considers that the Class I Stones go back to the Iron Age period.

I would agree with his sentiment, and would also suggest that some of these Class I Stones may go back to an even earlier period to the early builders of the megalithic tombs, which I will attempt to prove in this book. One group of symbol stones to assist in proving my theory is the Class I Logie Symbol Stones of Inverurie, Aberdeenshire.

Figure 76 *Stones forming an isosceles triangle.*

The Logie Class I Symbol Stones of Inverurie comprise three symbol stones forming an isosceles triangle (Fig. 76). These stones depict the seal, and have zoomorphic and geometric designs etched upon them. The apex stone (Fig. 77) is one of the most exciting of Scotland's Symbol Stones, imaging a series of geometric designs which give us a basic understanding of the early culture of the people. This stone viewed from the rear, as shown in this photograph, illustrates a large head of the seal that has not been previously noted; rotate the photograph anti-clockwise and examine the outline of the stone and observe the lozenged eye, with the shadowy snout and closed mouth of a large seal head.

Taking a more in-depth look at the front of this stone, I observed a further seal's head which I had not previously discussed or the true significance and importance of which at that time I had not realised and appreciated. The image of the head and the eye of the seal is only just discernible, as shown on the linen rubbing, but is a little clearer on the photograph (Fig. 79).

The central stone on the right of the apex stone (Fig. 76) is portraying a 'V' shape aperture, depicting the beginning, and the arrival of another seal. These stones image the seals as a united and committed group stretching skywards.

Figure 77 *Linen rubbing of the Logie Stone.*
By kind permission of Marianna Lines

The symbols on this stone have been highlighted by taking a linen rubbing, using vegetable dyes in order not to damage the stone or its incised symbols. The linen rubbing was taken by artist Marianna Lines, who has produced many fine rubbings of Scotland's symbol stones. This stone has been referred to as a sun-god, which it is, but it also portrays the seal as the main sacred sea-creature for these early people in Britain and Ireland. Note the outline shadow of a 'V' just protruding through the linen positioned above the sun's rays, indicating an open mouth as shown on Figure 78, Ref. D.

The symbols highlighted by the linen rubbing can be at first a little daunting to interpret. In order to simplify these symbols the following layout has been prepared to assist readers to evaluate this stone for themselves:

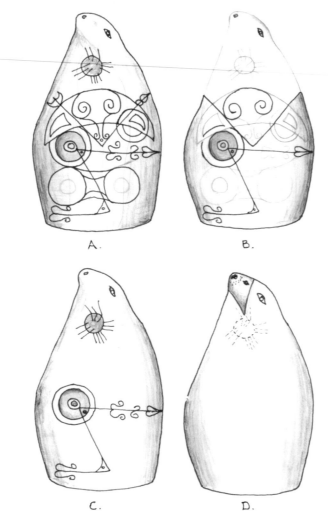

Figure 78 *Logie Stone symbols.*

Ref. A

The Logie Stone, Ref.A, is confirming that the sun had played a main part in early people's worship to the heavens above. The short lines emanating from the small circle near the top of the stone mark the rays of the sun. Some consider the lines to represent the Irish Ogham letters, however I believe this idea to be fanciful and misleading. The sun did indicate that the tribe looked to the heavens for guidance, but the rays of the sun are also indicating the whiskers appearing from the snout of a seal.

This stone may be traced back to megalithic times, and is a fine example of the record of our early history relating to various stages of tribal integration progressing from Mesolithic to Neolithic times to the Bronze Age, Iron Age, and on to the acceptance of Christianity. The 'V' and 'Z' symbols had in early Neolithic times been simple plain line figures without the decoration of the arrow head and lappets, both symbols indicating 'the beginning'. It was not until later, with the arrival of Christianity, that the arrow lappet features were possibly considered to indicate that by breaking the tribal war arrow/lance they were indeed breaking away from old tribal customs and traditions and accepting a new Christian Faith.

These two symbols were possibly the only symbols altered by the Picts on Scotland's Class I stones, in order to record and confirm this new faith, and the change taking place in the control of a tribe being transferred from the ladies in a matriarchal society to a male ruling system. This transfer of power can be seen with the arrow bisecting the crescent within which is the head of a sheep, shown in the form of scrolls; these scrolls may also refer to the seal's flippers, depicted within the crescent.

The acute angles formed by the arrow and the lance are two of the oldest symbols of Mesolithic man representing 'A' for 'alpha', the beginning. It is also worth noting, within a small triangular shape inside the acute angles of the arrow and the lance, the inclusion of an eye representing the head and eye of the seal.

The 'Z-Rod' is also bisecting the avenue-lined double henge, known as a double disc, representing a tribe from a stone henge, or a hill fort, and indicates the origin of a tribe and its evolution from the main stone circle; note that the apex of the 'Z'-Rod points to the inner-centre of the circle/eye. The outer periphery of the circle, itself over-lapped by the crescent belonging to the seal-tribe of their forefathers, also indicates that a direct tribal merger had taken place. There are other symbols that can be observed on this stone, but to prevent confusion they have not been included. All of these tribes had revered their forebears and illustrated their ancestral origins on stone.

Ref. B

This sketch illustrates the eye of a sea creature pin-pointed by the 'Z' -Rod possibly delineating the seal, with its mouth wide open as if swallowing the symbol of a sheep's head. However the open mouth may also be indicating the fundamental belief of these people that the whale created the seal, as shown, and confirms the similar beliefs held by people throughout the length and breadth of Britain and Ireland. The sheep's head may refer to the importance of farming as a further development of their economy. The influence of the farming community over the people is depicted by the sheep's head, shown centrally positioned within the symbol of the crescent as indicated in Ref. A. The overall outline symbol of the crescent stands for the seal with the two spirals as the side flippers; the crescent is also highlighting the two acute triangles representing the wedge shape formation of a tomb. The crescent can be allied to the seal as shown on the photograph of the seal swimming on its side just below the surface of the water (Colour Plate No.4).

Ref. C

There is a great deal more to this symbol stone than is at first apparent. The sun is representing a nostril, and its rays the whiskers of a seal. The eye of the seal is the circle, highlighted by the apex of the broken 'Z'-Rod pointing to the centre of a stone circle. Turn the sketch to the right and look at the overall shape of the stone in relation to the eye and the whiskered nostril, and it can clearly be seen as the head of a seal.

Ref. D

The overall shape of the stone is a seal encompassing the sun within its heart. However there is an even older sculptured symbol of the 'V' shaped mouth, from which a seal is emerging (Fig. 80) directly relating to the megalithic stones portraying the selfsame beginning of the life of a seal, with the 'V' shape of the mouth attesting to the early symbol of 'A' for 'alpha'.

Figure 79 *Logie Seal Stone.*

The other two symbol stones can also take on the shape of seals depending on the angle from which they are viewed. The influence of Egyptian art and beliefs may have been introduced by the incoming farming communities as they tried to combine some of their own beliefs with those of the indigenous people. Egyptians believed that the bird came down from the sun to take the spirit of the deceased back up to the heavens. This idea may well have been introduced by travellers from the eastern Mediterranean.

Figure 80 *Seal lying prostrate across the top of the stone.*

There is a sculptured seal lying flat across the top of this stone, its small curved head lying to the top left, the eye clearly observed and its snout positioned just like that of a dog stretched in front of a fire. Other groups of seals not so readily discernible are sculptured on the right hand vertical side. These seals appear to be gambolling on the rocks on the shore. The general overall shape of this stone is a seal, similar to the orthostats, the top left hand corner indicating the upturned snout, while on the top right hand side is the radius of the seal's large curved head, with the eye encompassed within a small triangle.

It is normal for people looking at this stone for the first time to observe the two inscribed symbols referred to as the 'Swimming Elephant' and the crescent bisected with the 'V'- Rod. The 'Swimming Elephant' is a bird of the grebe family and may well be the merganser, quite common in this area. Adding this bird to the symbol stone indicates a connection with Egypt, and Horus the falcon, who was believed to carry aloft the spirit of the departed from their burial chambers, such as the Pyramids of Egypt.

Figure 81 *Merganser, the Sea Goose.*

This bird normally searches the water for small fish as part of its diet. The bird shown on this stone (Fig. 81) is hovering over and looking down upon the bisected crescent shape of a seal, which may represent a burial place. This burial chamber is indicated by the acute triangular shape appearing at the ends of the crescent, and may refer to the triangular plan view of these three upright Logie Stones.

It has been sugested that the spiral of this bird running up and over its head and along its back represented an elephant's trunk, hence the reference to it as a 'swimming elephant'. If one looks carefully at this bird it can be established that the spiral is sprouting from the top of the head and not from the mouth, as it would have done if the creature were an elephant; the spiral is in fact the curled head-comb of a water-goose.

The other spirals positioned directly behind the bird's beak represent the bird's wings in the downward position of flight. The rear spiral indicates that the bird can swim under water. This spiral shape is also used to identify the lower body rear spiral flippers of the sacred seal, as observed in Figure 24.

Figure 82 *Crescent of the Seal.*

The overall shape of this stone can also portray a seal similar to those used for orthostats, ie. the snout on the left hand side assists in holding the capstone aloft. Depicted on this stone is the crescent bisected by the broken arrow. The broken arrow is a development from the old triangle meaning 'A' for 'alpha'. Note the eye of the seal at the top right hand side highlighted by the smaller curved triangle placed within the acute angle.

The crescent shape represents the seal (*see* Fig. 91) and may refer to a plan view of a ceremonial burial site. Note the crescent also depicts the inscribed spiral flippers of the seal, along with an obtuse angle, which is similar to those markings found on the actual seal. The double disc may suggest the amalgamation of the people from a double henge with those of the seal tribe.

Machrie Moor, Island of Arran

To obtain further proof of our forefathers' belief that the seal had held the spirit of our ancestors, I retraced my steps back to the area of my own roots to the Firth of Clyde, journeying on by ferry to the grandeur of the mountains and glens of the beautiful Island of Arran, around which the Gulf Stream ebbs and flows with each successive tide.

Figure 83   *Seal Menhir of Machrie Moor.*

The impact on the landscape of the Island of Arran over many, many years of human occupation has been profound. Machrie Moor is especially rich in Mesolithic, Neolithic and Bronze Age remains, dating to at least 5500 years ago. The site of a stone circle is still marked by three exceptionally massive pillars of red sandstone, standing proudly as if on guard over a number of other fallen stones. The tallest of the three is 18 feet in height, while the stone shown in Figure 83 is just over 13 feet and is of particular interest portraying the large head of a seal looking pensively to the skies. The early people of Arran may well have agreed with the last lines of the song 'Though my eyes look to the skies, I lift my heart to heaven.' The seal was not perceived as a god, but as a sacred link in the chain of evolution of man in relation to God, who in turn had created all living things in the sea and on the land.

On Arran are the remains of at least ten stone circles, including an oval ring of six roughly dressed slabs of red sandstone, along with numerous standing stones, and an interesting selection of Clyde-type burial cairns. These cairns also depict symbols of the seal and help to confirm that the people looked upon the seal as a sacred creature. The many stones and ancient burial sites on the island indicate that a large community had lived and worked here. The sea played a major link with the other inhabitants of the West Coast of Scotland, and with Ireland, and also provided a very important trading partnership with their fellow-man in Wessex.

Further trading connections can be established with the mining of copper and with the jet crescentic necklace shown in Figure 87, similar to the Baltic amber necklaces found in Southern England. The techniques used by the people building Stonehenge with its tongued and grooved joints were also applied in the construction work on some of the sides of the short cists found on the island.

On Machrie Moor one comes across many stone circles, several of which were the circular foundations of ancient dwelling places. This area had at one time been an integral part of the ancient stone culture, where some stones were cut in a circular shape from boulder rock and a square hole cut and positioned in the centre; these may have been used as a wheel for a cart or wagon, or simply as a grinding wheel for cereals.

Figure 84 *The view from Machrie Moor.*

Figure 84 shows one of the many smaller standing stones which were erected overlooking the sea. This stone had a carving of a seal positioned vertically on the centre of the stone, which in its own right is shaped as the sacred seal looking to the skies. The smaller boulder to the left of the picture has also inscribed lines of the head of the seal shown upon it, and may represent the overseer.

These enigmatic abstract geometric symbols, some overlain by other motifs, have given rise to a great deal of speculation leading to debate as to their significance and purpose; so far no conclusive answers have yet been given! It becomes apparent to me that these early people, unable to read or write, were attempting to leave a message for future generations, just as the Americans have attempted to send into orbit details of our present day life and culture enclosed within a space capsule.

Our ancient ancestors had obviously discussed with one another the source of origin of man. Their findings were then directly linked to their early religious beliefs, which related to rebirth and regeneration.

The people of Wessex, who erected the standing stones at Windmill Hill, Avebury Henge, and Stonehenge, had at least one thing in common with the rest of the people in Britain and Ireland, and that was their dedication to the sacred seal. It would appear that in every settlement they had stones which portrayed the seal. The men portrayed the seal with geometric symbols on their axes, shields, weapons, standing stones, funerary ware and in the sacred ceremonial burial sites. Their flints shaped as a crescent and depicting the seal were possibly early tokens used as bargaining counters in their early economy.

This new economy based on mining and refining copper, tin, gold, silver, and other metals, can be observed as an expanding export industry, producing ingots in the shape of their own fundamental religious beliefs. This can be observed on the rectangular metal ingots, where the acute 'V' shape formation had been cast into either end of the ingot to lighten the block significantly and also assisted in the physical lifting and handling of these metal bars.

Further prosperity followed as ladies wore crescent shaped gold collars and owned bronze and copper hand-mirrors, displaying the sacred seal. Men would wear an open torc around their necks even in battle, and the women an open bracelet, the gap representing the entrance to the sacred henge, circle or burial tomb. These people assumed that, if they died or were killed, the wearing of these forms of jewellery would ensure their smooth passage to immortality in a new life after death. The seal was at the hub of their economy and at the very heart of their ceremonial rituals held at open air enclosures, hilltop retreats and sacred burial sites. It is stated in the old culture of the Chinese that there is a beginning and an end to everything. These early people believed implicitly in a new spiritual regeneration.

CHAPTER 8
Ancient Triangular Art Designs

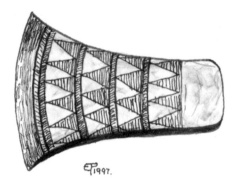

Figure 85 *Danish axe head.*
After I. McNeil Cooke

*A*cute angles or triangles can also be traced to Europe to a Danish Axe Head, where the basic triangular design has been incorporated in this Bronze Age artwork of the Axe Head. The triangles represent the heads of seals separated by vertical lines indicating the water from which the heads appear. Triangles are depicted on jewellery, war shields, and on Beaker funerary vessels.

The word 'vessels' leads me to our important maritime culture of importing and exporting beakers, which may be associated with the Beaker movement, a subject in its own right. My quick appraisal of the designs of the all-over Corded Bell Beakers from Europe and the Mediterranean does not signify that Britain was being over-run by people from other lands; on the contrary our ports had been at the forefront of exporting our minerals, and importing and exporting other goods such as funerary urns, and animal skins. The latest improvements in the make-up of these vessels were based on the updated triangular designs, part of an ever expanding religious economy sweeping through Western Europe and the Mediterranean.

The large triangular and diamond pattern designs, as shown on Beaker pottery, can be traced back in time from the late Neolithic period to the early Bronze Age stages of Beaker ware in Britain. This indicates to me that the development of this pottery was based upon social demands, related to the religious beliefs of the people of Britain, Ireland, and of Western Europe.

The triangle is also a prominent feature of the design of the crescentic seal necklaces worn by the ladies of fashion during the Bronze Age. These necklaces were exported to the Mediterranean area and became a thriving business. Many books written by authors of ancient Roman history refer to the jet necklaces manufactured in Britain and exported to Europe and the Mediterranean countries.

The triangle eventually became one of the symbols with which the early Christian missionaries had to contend. Their reference to the triangle as the Holy Trinity would in all likelihood differ from the interpretation put on it by the local people. However, as will be found, the triangle played a major role in the building of our early churches, and can be seen on some of our churches even to this day.

Crescentic Seal Necklaces

The triangular shape had been selected by Neolithic people of Britain as a simple design to illustrate the head of the sacred seal on their jewellery.

The triangle appears on the reconstructed fragments of a crescentic jet necklace taken from a chamber incorporated into a byre wall at Tormore Farm, Island of Arran. What struck me, when completing the following sketch of the crescentic necklace, is its similarity to the design of the crescent inscribed on the Logie Stone. This is no mere coincidence, as when one looks carefully at both designs they bear a very close resemblance and incorporate the triangular motifs found within the apex head of the crescent of the Logie Stone, both designs relating to the seal.

Figure 86 *Reconstructed crescentic Arran necklace.*

The development of the Arran necklace can be appreciated, when studying the following sketch of the Ross-shire Jet necklace, found in Northern Scotland. Cross plates have been added to the set of irregular oval jet beads, which are strung together like our modern jewellery.

Figure 87 *Artist's sketch of the Ross-shire jet necklace.*

As a symbol of early people's faith and their respect for the seal the ladies of the Bronze Age wore crescentic necklaces which represented the saltire design and the crescentic-shaped body of the sacred seal, whereas some ladies today wear a crucifix.

At Mountstuart House, on the Island of Bute, Firth of Clyde, there is yet a further development of the sacred seal necklace made from beautiful jet beads and plates, dating back to 2000–1600BC, the all-important triangles and diamond designs, as well as 'A' for 'alpha', inscribed at the ends of each jet plate.

Figure 88 *Jet crescentic plate necklace.*

The people of Wessex, who were also seal worshippers, had established trading settlements on the islands of Arran and Bute, in the estuary of the River Clyde. They were miners and overseers of the shipments of copper obtained from the Kilmartin valley, Argyll. Evidence of this close cultural relationship with Wessex man can be related to a dagger found at Blackwaterfoot, Arran. This dagger has a close affinity to the first phase of the Wessex culture, dated 1910–1600BC.

It becomes apparent that the ladies of the Bronze Age, like the ladies of today, were fashion-conscious, as they wore jet seal crescentic necklaces in Northern Britain, and amber seal crescentic necklaces in Southern Britain. The museum at Devizes, Wiltshire, displays a Baltic amber crescentic necklace, which had been found in Wiltshire. This necklace is complete with its triangular decorated shaped amber head and amber cross plates. It is similar to the overall design of the Bute jet crescentic necklace.

The crescentic design of the seal can be seen on the Lunula Gold Collar necklaces found throughout Britain and Ireland. The overall crescent formation has led to the name 'lunula', providing only a tenuous link to the moon.

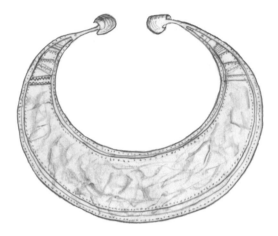

Figure 89 *Sanquhar gold collar.*

The crescentic beaten gold sheet collar with incised decoration, Fig.89, came from Auchentaggart, Dumfriesshire, dated c.2000 BC. It had been designed to have the natural catenary sag to form the graceful outline of the seal, and has nothing whatsoever to do with the moon. The craft of goldworking can be found in Britain and Ireland along with copper working. The Lunulae collars are considered to have originated in Ireland.

These crescentic designs follow the same basic natural curved shape of the crescent inscribed on the Logie Stone. The association has now been shown, I trust, between the Logie Stone and the crescentic necklaces, including the triangular headed design, which is akin to the Baltic amber seal crescentic necklaces manufactured in Southern England. These designs are not just vaguely but strikingly similar to those found in Mycenae, Crete, where links can also be made to the multiple lozenge designs, which, I believe, had been introduced earlier to Crete by the seal tribes from Western Europe.

Many brooches depicting the seal were manufactured in Britain and Ireland, yet until now no one has ever even considered relating the crescent shape of the brooch to the seal. The Hunterston Brooch, found at

Hunterston, West Kilbride, Ayrshire, is a fine example of Pictish metal work, shown in Figure 90. The fabulous intricate art-design of the Gael shows a very high standard of craftsmanship depicted on this crescent shape brooch. The layout of this crescentic annular brooch with its triangular terminals is akin to the inscribed crescent appearing on the Logie Stone, both highlighting the wedge design of a burial chamber, along with the all-important circle of a henge. The entrance to the henge is shown on this brooch by the two sets of circular studs placed on either side of the pin to indicate pillars placed on each side of the entrance passageway, similar to the entrance to Mayburgh Henge (Fig. 58).

Figure 90 *Hunterston Brooch, Ayrshire.*
© Trustees of the National Museums of Scotland, 1998

The interwoven spirals produced by the Gael are highlighted on the artwork of the Hunterston Brooch as sea-creatures, that appear to be swimming at speed like the seal, darting here and there through the water with their mouths in some cases wide open. In the lower centre of the outer periphery and on the inner lower central curve of the brooch there are four seals curving in towards one another. In the following photograph, Figure 91, the curved camouflaged body of the seal can be observed and studied as it basks in the mid-day sun.

Figure 91 Basking seal.

The curved figure of the basking seal once again illustrates the truly fascinating camouflaged body of this mammal. Note the small lozenge shape around its ear hole, and the larger diamond pattern formed on the body, whilst the tail flippers are curled up in a bunch as if they are the heads of seal pups. Within this tail configuration one can observe the shape of a life-size styled seal head. This gives us a better understanding of why there are two curved seal heads on jewellery, and as portrayed on standing stones and in burial sites. From the spotted body pattern there are many shapes of seal heads that one can visualise, which assisted in confusing a predator such as Orca, the whale.

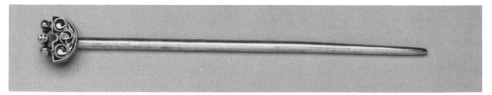

Figure 92 Pictish silver hand pin.
© Trustees of the National Museums of Scotland, 1998

This 6th–7th century Pictish silver hand pin, with the overall crescent formation of the seal, was found at Norrie's Law, near Largo, Fife. The crescent has been decorated with red enamel providing a background to the fine spiral design representing the eyes and the snout of the seal. On the reverse side there is an incised Pictish symbol of a 'Z'- rod. At the top of this pin is a motif of the cross which had earlier indicated a pagan round barrow, and is now looked upon as a Christian Cross. On either side of the cross are the circular symbols imaging the round barrow. Within the crescent of the seal are the two circles of the round barrow, which also indicate the eyes of the seal, with the central circle representing its snout.

A few miles from Largo, at the scenic fishing harbour of Crail, recent excavations on a golf course have revealed a number of pits containing tiny flint tools, and burned hazelnut shells; radiocarbon dates indicate a period of 9500 years ago. Dr. Stephen Carter of Headland Archaeology has said -

'practically all the flints belong to a single type – 'crescent' type microliths, shaped like a half moon – whereas on repeated occupation of sites a collection of different types is generally found.'

The crescentic shape is interesting as it raises further speculation. The tiny microliths were known to form the cutting edge of a tool, and these crescentic shapes may also have been used as a form of token to barter for other goods. These microliths may have represented the curved body of the seal, and give more credence to their use as cultural tokens in a Middle Stone Age economy.

What specially interests me about these pits found on the golf course at Crail is the lack of permanent dwellings, other than a camp site. This camp site was possibly used during the summer months to manufacture microliths, which were assembled to become cutting implements, or cultural seal charms and tokens. In the winter months during the colder weather these people may have retreated to caves on the coast, similar to the nearby Wemyss Caves at East Wemyss, Fife. Frank Rankin, in his *Guide to the Wemyss Caves*, 1993, states - **'In fact there are more markings in the Wemyss Caves than in all the caves in Britain put together'.** His sketches made on site are indeed of interest, and should be followed up and accurately recorded by academics.

These inscribed symbols are fascinating. Some are said to relate to the symbols appearing on the Pictish Class II Stones! Some of these symbols do appear on the symbol stones of Scotland, and here I believe that these symbolic stones can be traced back to the Neolithic period and possibly even earlier. These symbols were known by the Picts who inscribed them on their Class II Stones. This may then assist us to establish that the Picts can trace their ancestry back to one of the earliest groups to inhabit Britain.

One scene is said by Frank Rankin to be a hunting scene! To me this is an inscribed symbol of the sacred seal shown as in Fig. 93 A; there are also two different symbols indicating 'omega', one with the eyebrow symbol, the other just above it to the left looks like the letter 'W', possibly an even older 'omega' symbol, which eventually was used by the Greeks as the small letter 'w' for omega. Colour Plate No.9 illustrates a seal in the water with its pronounced triangular eyebrows, and may confirm that the symbolic 'W' was derived by early people.

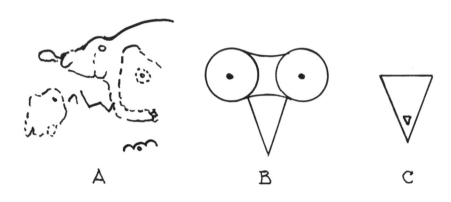

Figure 93 *Wemyss Cave Carvings, Fife.*
After F. Rankin

The centre symbol (Fig. 93 B) shows a double disc and an earlier form of the 'V'-Rod. This symbol to me suggests two Round Barrows or henges (the eyes of a seal), with the 'V' indicating the entrance to the beginning of a new life (the tapered snout of the seal) associated with the two barrows, which are also linked by an avenue. The symbol illustrated in Figure 93 C, is said to be an unidentified marking! This I recognise as the triangle 'delta', the symbol of the head of the seal, which is inverted in this instance and indicates the resting place of an individual; the main triangular design includes a smaller triangle indicating the eye of the seal. This triangular symbol in time would have been incorporated into the gable wall of the early church, followed later by the addition of steeples.

Figure 94 *Newgrange Recumbent Stone.*

The 'W' symbol also appears on one of the recumbent stones found encircling the Newgrange Mound, in Ireland. Within the triangular design of the 'W' are the faint outlines of a seal's head. The origin of this 'W' symbol goes back to the two lozenge shapes that appear around the eyes of the seal (Fig. 64) which form in this instance an inverted type symbol of the eyebrow, with the twin apex of the 'W' symbol pointing to the ground indicating a resting place for the departed, 'omega' the end. This recumbent stone in its own right depicts a seal; note its rounded head on the far right hand side and the small lozenge which is enclosed within a slightly larger triangle indicating the eye and the head of a seal looking down to the ground. The opposite end also shows the seal looking to the left with its small lozenge shaped eye. There are many lozenge shapes present on this stone along with other smaller heads.

Multi-serrated type symbols are also incorporated in the passageway of a tomb as shown inscribed on the bone hand-comb design (Fig. 47). This saw-tooth type of art work is a feature found on the decorated stone that had at one time been located behind the Bryn Celli Ddu Burial Chamber, Anglesey, the original stone now housed in the National Museum of Wales.

Figure 95 *Decorated stone.*
By kind permission, Cadw Welsh
Historic Monuments

The Bryn Celli Ddu Burial Chamber
– the Mound in the Dark Grove – appears to
have commenced as a henge or as a ritual enclosure, with a stone circle surrounded by a
bank and internal ditch. This was partially
integrated latterly as a passage grave. This
tomb is said to be one of the most evocative
archaeological sites in Britain. The decorated
curvilinear stone found at Bryn Celli Ddu
Burial Chamber (Fig. 95) is very similar to
the adorned symbol stones found in Ireland
and in Brittany. The inner passageway along
the length of the tomb is of particular interest as it highlights the skills of the masons
who incorporated the heads of seals within
the construction of the stone walls.

There are two sculptured heads of a seal
shown clearly on the lower section of the projected stone; there are also
other heads to be seen. The head on the left hand side of the stone projection is just outwith the upper decoration looking diagonally upwards to
the left, and the one close to the right hand side of the stone is looking
diagonally downwards to the right. The convoluted pattern has both the
eyebrow and the saw-tooth design incorporated as a flowing outline of a
river or stream, indicating the water of life, depicted as a passage tomb
leading to an inner chamber. The chamber is the outline of the seal and
can best be observed when inverting the photograph. A number of the
curved or serrated outlines also incorporate the head of the seal within the
design. The decoration on this stone is referring to a burial chamber,
whether the one at this particular site or another is a matter for conjecture.

Inside the chamber one of the stones on the south side has an inscribed
spiral design carved on it. These decorated stones can also be found on
many other Welsh and Irish sites illustrating the eyebrow and convoluted
patterns. These designs are also common to Ireland, and can be found on
sculptured stone monuments at Newgrange, Knowth and other tombs in
the Boyne Valley, yet the significance of these decorated patterns has not
been fully realised.

The tomb at Barclodiad y Gawres, in Anglesey, has also a series of decorated curvilinear designs with spirals, eyebrows and lozenge patterns included on the sculptured stones, as shown in Figure 96.

Figure 96 *Seal Chamber.*

This rock art style has been said to be abstract, possibly due to the fact that people had forgotten or did not understand the significance of these fascinating designs, which were known and clearly understood by Neolithic people.

These decorated stones have been said by Cadw Welsh Historic Monuments to mark the boundary between the world of the living and that of the spirits of the dead. As far as I am aware no one has attempted to explain how these designs indicate this spiritual interpretation, with which, I hasten to say, I agree. I will now attempt to qualify their reasoning.

The overall shape of the stone is that of a sculptured seal portrayed as if giving birth to a pup. The aperture of the tail represents 'A' the beginning, and in the chamber below the 'W' indicates 'omega' the end, as well as water. (Egyptian Pharaohs during their journey in the underworld also travelled over water before being transferred to the heavens.) At the base of the sculptured seal stone is the entrance to a passageway with the boulder constructed avenue highlighting the curved stalls and cells of the eyebrow curvilinear pattern. Each curved stall or cell also indicates the head of a seal, as the last resting place for the dead, emphasised by the spiritual lozenge design.

This lozenge design is the seal's head looking downwards and upwards, indicating the arrival of the spirit of the dead at the tomb and also indicates the next stage of its journey upwards through the open 'V' shaped type aperture representing the 'beginning', the regeneration of the spirit as a seal. The next phase is the emergence of a seal from this aperture to continue its spiritual journey in the new world in the heavens.

CHAPTER 9
The Early Culture of Wessex

*I*n Wessex the considered classic Neolithic enclosure for Southern Britain is of course Windmill Hill, as it was one of the first to be excavated and finds from it have been thought to be typical of the Earlier Neolithic period. It was first occupied in c.3800 BC, yet it only came to be noticed in the early years of this century by the vicar of Winterbourne Monkton, the Rev. Kendall, who found many examples of scatters of flint and pottery. Early in 1920, the archaeologist, O.G.S.Crawford, became aware of plans to erect a Marconi wireless station on the hill, and informed Alexander Keiller, who was interested as an amateur archaeologist. Keiller was also heir to the Keiller marmalade and jam factories in Dundee, Scotland.

Keiller examined Windmill Hill from the air and then in 1924–25 bought the site. Excavations began first under the directions of H.St.George Gray, and then by Keiller himself. Two separate phases were identified, an Earlier Neolithic pre-enclosure settlement of c.3700BC, and the Middle Neolithic causewayed camp. Further excavations were carried out by Isobel Smith in 1957–58 to clarify the sequence of the ditches and obtain dating and surroundings samples. A further re-excavation was carried out by Dr. A. Whittle, Cardiff University, in 1988. Some of the pottery was found to have originated in Cornwall and Frome, along with stone axes which came from Cumbria, Cornwall and Wales.

Upon studying the plan view I decided to redraw it in relation to the two barrows positioned in line with one another (*see* Fig. 94). People today refer to a square enclosure positioned between two round barrows, however this was not how the ancients looked upon it. As in the first instance they had intended it to be a lozenge shaped enclosure or diamond pattern this would have been the Neolithic design for the enclosure.

The lozenge configuration, as found at Newgrange, indicated the resting-place for the dead. Scholars have rightly surmised that the Windmill enclosure had possibly been used for exposing human remains prior to final burial.

There are a number of interesting thoughts that can be expressed regarding this lozenge shape in relation to Windmill Hill. First the lozenge design represents the open mouth of a seal placed between the two round barrows which form the all-seeing eyes of the seal. This design can be seen inscribed on the stones found at Newgrange, and also on jewellery. This layout is located to the east just outside the main outer perimeter of the Windmill Henge. I believe that this enclosure represented the ceremonial catchment area for the newly deceased who were placed within the lozenge enclosure to witness the first light of day as part of the ceremony of transferring the spirit of the departed to a new after-life. Windmill Hill is of course older than the Castlerigg Stone Circle, where they had brought the enclosure of the sanctuary within the confine of the circle as opposed to it being positioned outside the henge.

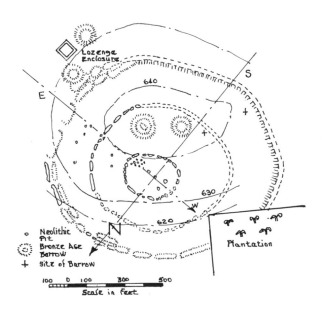

Figure 97 Windmill Hill Enclosure.

The overall shape of this enclosure is intended to represent a frontal view of a seal, with the second inner circle depicting the head and the two barrows as the eyes, while the central circle is the snout, and the entire outer shape indicates the circular body of the seal. This layout of the front view of a seal, like many others, was to be observed from the skies by their god. Britain is not unique in having animal and human figures that can be observed from the air. Even in the Continent of America large animal and scroll figures from ancient times have been recorded by aerial photography.

On studying the aerial view of Windmill Hill causewayed enclosure (not illustrated), photographed in 1949 by the University of Cambridge, I observed several outlines of seal heads in the central ring, and outwith the causeway some located on the inclined slopes of the hill. The crescent and other acute angles are also present in what appears to have been a very large settlement in the area of this hill, which is 640 ft. above sea level and is located 1 mile north-west of Avebury.

Neolithic Avebury

The Menhirs of Neolithic Avebury constitute one of the most intact pre-historic complexes to be found in Europe, and had formed until recently the largest known henge in Britain, with an average internal diameter of 385' 6", and an external diameter of 474' 4". The henge is dated c.2900–2600BC and it has the remains of two smaller circles approximately 350 feet in diameter, referred to as the northern inner circle, and the southern inner circle which has a 'D' formation forming the eye of the seal. It is intriguing that the earlier ditches had been 'V' shaped in section. The tools employed in the excavation of the site were antler picks and rakes, with wooden shovels and baskets for the removal of material.

It was John Aubrey, the antiquarian, who came across the forgotten stones whilst out hunting in 1649. He did not excavate the site which he considered to be the premier ancient site in Britain, but later he wrote ' it does as much exceed in greatness the so renowned Stonehenge, as a ca-thedral doeth a parish church'. Some 60 years later William Stukeley, doc-tor and cleric, came to Avebury to study the site. Shortly after this demol-ishers began to break up the stones creating massive damage.

Stukeley made a sketch recording the stone-burning at Avebury in 1724. Straw had been heaped around the stones in a large pit, and water poured over the heated stones to crack them, then finally they were broken up with sledge-hammers. The surviving parts of the Avebury Circles and avenue were mainly reconstructed, due once again to the amateur archae-ologist, Alexander Keiller, who purchased this site and traced many of the stones that had lain buried for many years, some since mediaeval times. In 1934-35, he arranged for the excavation in the circle, and the re-erection of the stones in their original positions.

Figure 98 Avebury Seal.

Figure 98 illustrates the heads of two seals. The first view of this stone indicated the seal with its head and snout proudly lifted upwards to the skies to the right. When studying the photograph the three deep sockets depicted the deep sunken eyes and the open mouth of the seal. Sadly this stone even today has been vandalised by the addition of painted daubed symbols.

Figure 99 *Avebury Seal Head.*

This stone (Fig. 99) portrays the head of the seal clearly positioned, looking to the left, with its triangular eye in the centre near the top of the stone. This is a stone of immense proportion as readers will observe. The seal head can be traced to many of the stones in this complex.

Two other stones at Avebury confirm that both represent the seal. When examining the right hand stone shown in Figure 100, carefully look for the incised lozenge shape design towards the right hand side, mid-way up the stone, where in the centre of the diamond is the eye of the seal, with its head raised upwards looking to the left to the sky. The tip of the raised snout of the seal is also enclosed within an inscribed lozenge shaped design. May I suggest that archaeologists examine what appears from my photographs to be an embedded orange type stone, located at the tip of the snout?

Figure 100 *The Beginning.*

In order to attempt to discuss some of these ancient designs which appear on this stone it is necessary to look carefully at sketches (Fig. 101) illustrating some of the more prominent shapes that can be observed, keeping in mind that some of these designs can and do overlap one another.

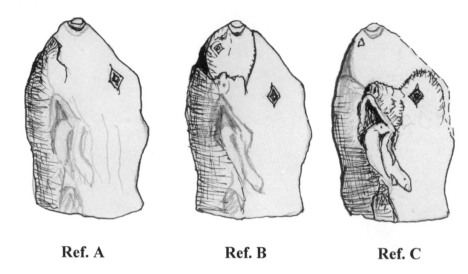

Ref. A   **Ref. B**   **Ref. C**

Figure 101 Designs on stone.

Ref. A: A seal looking pensively to the sky.

Ref. B: Here the sea-creature appears as if it has its mouth wide open and from its mouth emerges a seal. (There are several other heads of seals that can be observed within the mouth, but have not been included in this sketch.)

Ref. C: This is the one menhir which I have come across depicting the seal with its head and mouth open and seals moving in and out of the open orifice, as illustrated, indicating the beginning of a new life. There are several lozenge shapes located on this stone which represent the eyes of several other creations.

Referring back to Figure 100 the stone on the left has similar characteristics to the Castlerigg triangular stone (Fig. 56). If readers invert Figure 100 they will observe the head of the seal, as if standing on the ground. Bring the photograph back to its true position and observe at least nine seal heads on this stone. At first I had thought that this stone had been placed upside down, but then realised that it also portrays the very large open type mouth, faintly inscribed on this massive stone and shown in the following sketch (Fig. 102).

On Figure 102, the huge open 'V' shaped cavern of an aperture indicates 'A' for 'alpha', the 'beginning' of a new life for the departed. The spirits of the dead were manipulated by the High Priest and transferred, it was thought, into the spirits of seals.

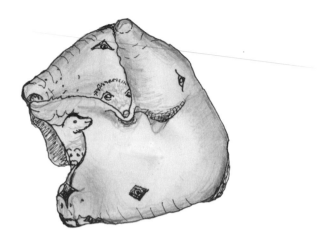

Figure 102 *The incredible beginning.*

This stone is actually depicting the birth of the seal which has its head to the ground and its tail raised skywards. If one studies yet again the photograph of the seals on the rock (Fig. 8) the camouflaged tail takes on the appearance of a seal's head with a closed mouth which also highlights a false eye (refer also to Fig. 14 & Fig. 91). This may well be the solution to understanding why a head is depicted at the top of a menhir and also another located near ground level.

Although the Avebury Circle can be traced back to c.2600BC, it is found that the religious ceremonies carried out at Avebury can also be linked to Windmill Hill, and to West Kennet Long Barrow, both erected c.3700BC. This date can be rather important and may illustrate that these early people may have influenced or been in contact with the Egyptians in relation to their religious ceremonies. One such Egyptian ceremony, known as the 'Opening the Mouth and Eyes', can be linked to our menhirs, such as Figure 102. This had been a special ritual performed by the Egyptians of the Old Kingdom on statues whereby the mouth and the eyes of the statue were anointed and touched with special utensils to enable it to receive the spirit of the departed at the moments of offering. This ceremony was continued into the New Kingdom in tomb chapels, and on the coffin of Butehamun of the early 21st dynasty, and carried on Papyri from Saqqara of early Roman times; this ceremony was used as a funerary text to ensure the revival of the deceased. At Akhmim an early demotic composition, the Book of Opening the Mouth for Breathing, combined the two principal concerns of that period into a single funerary text.

West Kennet Long Barrow

The West Kennet Long Barrow is one of the best-preserved burial chambers in Britain, and had been interpreted as the 'Archdruid's barrow' by Stukeley, who had linked the ancient stones romantically with the Druids and classical gods. As far as I am aware the Druids and other groups of today are quite unaware of the significance of the homage at one time paid to the seal.

When the tomb was in use, the entrance would have been in the form of a crescent shape forecourt, facing east, awaiting the rising of the sun. People may have gathered forming a circle as they carried out their ceremonial rituals to the deceased. Some 46 human skeletal parts had been buried on the floor of the chambers over a period of around 1500 years, from the first phase of the construction of the barrow, c.3700BC, until the Beaker period c.2000BC, when it has been said to have been finally sealed.

Figure 103 *Front view of West Kennet forecourt.*

Figure 103 illustrates the row of stones in front of the chamber, which assist in confirming the established and progressing religious beliefs of these early people. The largest central stone, referred to as a blocking stone, clearly shows the seal on the left hand side of the stone with its huge head and eye looking to the ground, and its flippered tail forming a 'V', to present yet another seal emerging to the heavens.

Figure 104 *West Kennet Forecourt Stone.*

The aerial view of the forecourt of the West Kennet Long Barrow, Colour Plate No.6, assists in confirming that these tombs were intended to be witnessed from the skies. Two boulders positioned at the top of the mound, one on either side of the modern concrete rectangular plinth, are a pair of overseers looking inwards, as well as looking in the opposite direction. On the centre of the so-called blocking stone is the seal looking diagonally upwards to the left, and it is also looking diagonally downwards to the right, similar to the design shown on the Sarsen Stone at Stonehenge (Fig. 112). The stone to the left on the forecourt is a seal looking to the right with its mouth open, highlighted by the shadow, while the remaining stones also portray the seal. Colour Plate No.6 indicates what may well be a further large head of a seal, as if it is emerging from the depths of the tomb, directly behind the two large frontal stones. This is a recurring ritual feature in burial chambers.

One of the last burials during the Beaker period was that of an elderly man, who had died with an arrow embedded in his throat. His complete skeletal remains were placed in a crouched position.

The large frontal ceremonial stone (Fig. 104) has the sculptured figures of two seal heads located at the top, as if lying in a prostrate position, one looking to the left and the other to the right. If readers carefully examine this stone they will find inscribed one very large seal-head its snout pointing to the ground, the eye highlighted by the 'V' positioned half-way up the stone and a third of the stone's width in from the left. There is a small boulder of the head of a seal lying on the ground to the left. To confirm the sculptured heads of seals at the top of this central stone a further photograph was taken of the opposite side of the stone looking east (Fig. 105).

Figure 105 *Rear View of Forecourt Stones.*

The frontal stone on the right in the background clearly depicts the sculptured heads of the seal; the lozenge shape can also be faintly traced at several locations, and several triangles relating to the 'beginning', within which are other inscribed seal heads. The large blocking stone on the left is representing the seal, with other seal heads faintly inscribed.

The seal had for many thousands of years been at the heart of religious rituals, which carried on through the Beaker period into the Christian period. Some of the pottery removed from this barrow was decorated with the lozenge pattern and some with the triangular designs of the seal, giving further proof of the long standing religious beliefs held by the people of Wessex.

Figure 106 *Funerary urn.*

The round pottery funerary urn, on which the triangle circumvents the circular interior, is further decorated with indented dimples cleverly included on the outer pattern to match the interior triangular design.

The triangular shape occurs naturally around the circular eye of a seal, the triangle on its own representing the head of the seal and the circle attesting to the eye. This design is one of the oldest symbols to be found, and is still to be seen to this present day.

It never ceases to amaze me how some people in our present civilisation with all its technology have apparently downgraded the intellect of our early ancestors. These early people were highly intelligent and were able to communicate with one another, were more than capable in debating the origin of their species, and possessed a profound knowledge of astronomy and nature.

Many scholarly books have been written stating that the people of Britain and Ireland had no written or documented language! Yet the people of Britain, and Ireland, like their counterparts in Western Europe, did have a symbolic form of recording their early culture, which they inscribed on rocks and tombs in the form of geometric and animal shapes, clearly understood by Neolithic man.

During the early part of 1997, a television series was screened on the subject of 'The Seven Wonders of the Ancient World.' In one of these programmes a wall panel carved in relief was shown. This panel was very difficult to read, due to age and weather deterioration, yet with modern technology the scenes on this panel were recreated and restored to show the original splendour. Use of this same technology should be considered today in order to illustrate the fascinating art culture inscribed on stones and boulders by our ancestors.

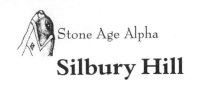

Silbury Hill

Silbury Hill is known as the largest man-built mound in Europe, standing 130 feet in height, with the outer wall leaning in at an angle of 60 degrees. After two centuries of investigation it has been said to be one of the most enigmatic prehistoric sites in Britain. Radiocarbon dating proposes that the first phase of construction goes back to c.2660BC. Silbury Hill had been built in three separate phases. In the last phase of construction six individual steps had been built of blocks of chalk, which led from the base to the top, encircling the pyramidal cone in ever-decreasing circular steps, where each step was 15–17 feet high, forming an intricate series of reinforced chalk walls. The steps were then infilled to present a smooth conical surface to the all-important empyrean.

In Southern England there is a tradition of using the chalk hills to illustrate figures intended to be seen from a distance as well as from above. This heritage applied to all of the megalithic chambers, such as Cairnholy I & II, Belas Knap, and West Kennet, where the seal mammal was presented to the celestial. This was an integral part of the ceremonial ritual, expressing implicit belief in a new life after death. These people were immersed both mentally and physically in their efforts to promote the seal to their god in the heavens. What better way to declare their faith than to have images of seals' heads incorporated as an integral design within the conical surface of Silbury Hill, where the images on the surface of the cone can be seen from every point of the compass.

A half mile to the east of Silbury Hill lies the Sanctuary, located on top of Overton Hill, where concrete posts now mark the three different phases of expansion which had taken place. This site had been excavated in 1930 by Maud Cunnington, who found that it had been built as a multiphase structure of three or four successive stages of construction.

The first wooden circular structure measured 15 ft. in diameter, and is said to have been constructed c.2800BC. This date has been arrived at due to the turf containing evidence of both flora and insect life appertaining to that period. The second phase had been the erection of a larger and more complex wooden circular building some 33 ft. in diameter. The third phase of expansion of this concentric structure was a larger building extending to some 65 ft. in diameter.

Figure 107 *Silbury Hill.*

The final phase saw the addition of two concentric rings of standing stones, one incorporated within the third phase of the circle and the other outwith the building. The outer ring of stones was connected by an entrance to the West Kennet Avenue on the north-west side, and marked the 'beginning' of the ceremonial processional route to a new life. It is possible that the terminally ill may also have been brought here to die in the mortuary of the Sanctuary. Later the remains of the dead were carried along a ceremonial route to Avebury Henge for the final transfer of their spirit, which coincided with the rising of the sun in the east. The privileged dead may then have been carried along a spiral path leading to the top of Silbury Hill, before being laid out to be viewed by the sun and the heavens, prior to being interred in either the Long Barrows or the Round Barrows. The spiral path, winding its way to the top of Silbury Hill, may indicate the update in their perception of their ancient plan views of spirals as inscribed on boulders. Note the triangle with the two indented eye type sockets, located on the left hand side at the base of this mound.

To the right is a lozenge design with the head and the eye of a seal looking to the left, located approximately a quarter way up from ground level. There are many other intriguing designs which can be observed on the surface of this man-made hill.

The date of the building of the first phase of Silbury Hill is rather interesting when compared with Egypt's stepped pyramid dated c.2630BC. In Wessex during construction a stepped conical pyramid was built to consolidate the shape of a cone to reach upwards to the skies. Egyptians during the Third Dynasty embarked on the building of a stepped pyramid at Saqqara, as they too wanted to get closer to their gods in the heavens. The stepped pyramid had been designed for King Djoser by his architect, Imhotep. This pyramid had been based on the principle of taking a large mastaba, and placing an ever smaller one on top, thus forming the pyramidal shape. It is also worth noting that many of the later pyramids had their surfaces given a smooth and flat finish rather than stepped, and that the pyramids are also triangular in shape.

Another fascinating link with Egypt is made with Osiris, who in one scene sat on his throne, at the base of which were panels displaying the ankh, the key of life. The ankh was the symbol of life carried by a Pharaoh during his reign, and on his death this was eventually handed over to Osiris in the underworld. Osiris, seated on his throne with his long acute tapering conical headgear, was also wearing a tight-fitting garment decorated with lozenge patterns, similar to those found on the body of a seal.

The lozenge design had been commonly used by the early megalithic people in Britain, Ireland and Western Europe. As mentioned earlier the significance of this diamond shape was to indicate the resting place of the dead, and Osiris was one of those deities responsible for ensuring the smooth transition of the spirit of the deceased from its resting place in the underworld to a new life and a new beginning in the empyrean. The lozenge design had also been cast on the handle of a ceremonial gold-bladed dagger tucked into a band found around the waist of Tutankhamen's body. Some mummy cases are also found to portray the symbolic lozenge pattern on their surface, indicating the resting place of the dead.

Another important link with the Eastern Mediterranean people had been made when Dolmens had been erected in Canaan. A further connection can be established with our Neolithic civilisation and the temple built at Karnak by Amenhotep IV, also known as Akhenaten, the sun worshipper, part of his name *naten* meaning the sun. He rejected the ancient gods of the Egyptians, in favour of paying homage to the sun. He was then despised by the Egyptians becoming known as the Heretic King. His wife, Nefertiti, shown on the back cover of this book, may have played an important role in his reign, especially in her support of sun worship. On the death of Akhenaten, the Egyptians returned to their old religious ways destroying the Temple of Karnak, which had been associated with his memory and life-style.

The spelling and the meaning of Karnak is similar to the name given to the rows of stones erected at Carnac in Brittany in France, and to the Gaelic word Carnac, meaning standing stones. The standing stones at Carnac in France were erected and aligned east-west to form the impressive passageway along which the spirit of the dead would be guided by the sun. The spirit of the deceased was eventually transferred as they thought to that of the seal, which welcomed the rising of the sun, and its departure to the west. Many of the standing stones at Carnac illustrate a seal appearing from the inscribed 'V' shaped aperture.

Silbury Hill with its flattened conical top was a ceremonial temple which at one time may have been level with the nearby West Kennet Long Barrow. It is quite apparent that the sacred Avebury Henge, Windmill Hill, the Sanctuary, East Kennet Long Barrow, and the many Round Barrows in the area were all integrated and linked by religious rituals and ceremonies. As these sites became redundant they were superseded by the ultimate pagan gathering-place built at Stonehenge.

In the November, 1997 issue, No. 29, British Archaeology, John Barrett in his article *Stonehenge, land, sky and the seasons* states:

'The question as to why Stonehenge was built is rather more complex. Most archaeologists become notably vague when questioned on this matter. It would appear from their vagueness, that we simply have to accept that complex societies, such as chiefdoms, build complex monuments.'

It would appear that the administrative heads of each ancient community were controlled or guided by a unifying force of sincere holy men, who in conjunction with the chiefdoms and the population held very strong religious beliefs and convictions, which motivated these ancient tomb-building societies.

These religious communities were at the very heart of a Stone Age economy, an economy that was an integral part of a wider system known throughout Western Europe, and the Mediterranean countries. Even in Thailand female ceremonial dancers wear a tight-fitting dress with lozenge design patterns, along with diamond patterned jewellery; they also wear tall acute conical headwear, pointing upwards to the skies.

Stonehenge

My close examination of Stonehenge was brief, being carried out after visitors had left, and within a period of thirty minutes before darkness fell. Stonehenge is the most enigmatic prehistoric monument in Britain.

Figure 108 Stonehenge.

This ancient ceremonial monument is quite unique not only in Europe, but throughout the rest of the world. There were three phases in the building of this henge. The first phase commenced as a large circular earthwork, used as a ceremonial gathering place about 5000 years ago. This was then followed by the second phase, which occurred between 2900–2600BC. Evidence found by archaeologists indicates that timber settings were added to the interior of the 'henge'. The third and final phase of Stonehenge began c.2600BC, with the arrival of the Blue stones from the Preseli Mountains in Wales, followed by the prodigious construction of the Sarsen Circle, and the ceremonial processional avenue which led to the beginning of a new spiritual life for the revered dead, as they began a journey of regeneration.

Archaeologists admit that they are unable to establish the original upright positions of many of these stones. This is possibly due to the large number of stones lying scattered around this monument. If they are seriously attempting to find the original place to erect all of these stones in a vertical position, then they do face an impossible task! Many of these stones were not, and were never intended to be, raised as standing stones, but were in fact recumbent stones depicting the seal, similar to the two recumbent stones shown in the foreground of the photograph of Stonehenge (Fig. 108). It may have been one of these recumbent stones that had been sculpted to show the twin tail of the seal. From this photograph the outline of the seal's head can be observed on the front face of the central stone with its spigot type-dowel protruding above the stone. The seal is also depicted on many other stones at Stonehenge.

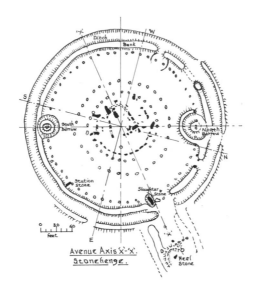

Figure 109 *General plan of Stonehenge today.*

The plan view of Stonehenge (Fig. 109) is portraying the frontal view of the seal's head, the South and North Barrows representing the eyes, and the horseshoe alignment of the sarsens and blue stones indicating the open mouth of the seal facing the avenue. From within the avenue the bank and ditch on either side of the entrance portray an open mouth, with the Heel Stone, the senior overseer, placed within a circle representing the eye and head of another symbolic seal, directly facing the opening of the inner henge.

Two sea-creatures facing each other with jaws wide apart is an integral feature of the ceremony of transferring a departed spirit from Stonehenge's processional avenue to the central area of the henge, depicted from the skies as the frontal view of the head of a seal with its mouth open. From here the spirit of the departed continued its spiritual journey with the awakening of the dawn in the east heralding the beginning of a new day and a new life, the spirit moving in harmony with the sun as it departed as one with the sun into the western horizon.

Figure 110 Reverse lower face of the Killamery Brooch.
By kind permission of the National Museum of Ireland

This same ceremonial feature is shown on the reverse side of the 9th. century Killamery brooch (Fig. 110) which is very revealing and can be directly affiliated to the layout of the circle and the alignment of stones forming the horseshoe configuration at Stonehenge. The reverse side of this Irish brooch clearly illustrates the head and open mouth of the seal attached to the circular annulus, indicating the henge. The open mouth of the seal faces the wedge-shape tomb, within which is a further seal with its mouth wide open forming a horseshoe shape, a pattern remarkably similar to that of the layout of Stonehenge (Fig. 109).

This annular seal brooch comes from Co.Kilkenny, Ireland, and has been cast in silver. The frontal view of this brooch (Fig. 111) illustrates the entrance to the circle with the two studs and a bar forming a gap indicating the passageway. The sunken lozenge shapes relate to the eye of a seal and to the lozenge design appearing on some occasions on the mitre worn by a bishop.

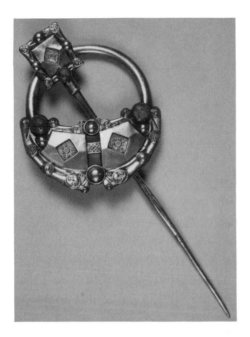

Figure 111 *Killamery Brooch.*
By kind permission of the National Museum of Ireland

Many other stones also portray the seal, including one of the blue stones called the 'Abbot's nose'. If one were to stand several yards back, towards the centre on axis X–X, Figure 109, and look in the direction of the blue stone of the seal, one can also observe to its right between the uprights of the two tall Sarsens the Heel Stone standing in the avenue in the distance. The Heel Stone from this position depicts two seal heads, one at the top of the stone, and another directly below with an open mouth. In the same direction the Slaughter Stone lies recumbent on the ground, and here again a seal's head can be found on the top positioned as if it were moving to greet the incoming spirit that had been ceremonially guided along the avenue to a new beginning.

When looking back and recalling the ancient portal dolmens, with their orthostats holding the quoit aloft, one can readily envisage the sarsen pillars as the orthostats at Stonehenge, supporting the lintels held up meaningfully to the skies. Neolithic people had come to the conclusion that a number of stones were required to encompass the circle to oversee the transfer of the departed to a new life. Stonehenge is a good example of this, as the people strove to be more accurate in their efforts in directing the spirit of the deceased along a predetermined path. New positive alignments were made, based on light from the sun and its shadow to guide and transfer the spirit of the deceased to a new happy afterlife.

It was believed that as the sun's rays shone into a tomb or passageway, the shining light assisted the regeneration of the dead to a new life. At Stonehenge they attempted to leave no space between the sarsens, as the lintel stones formed a solid continuous ring of curved seal stones held aloft in a protective and welcoming circle, barring evil influences during their ceremonies.

The importance of stone circles such as Stonehenge had a further impact on the economy, as jewellers began to perfect their art by glorifying their beliefs in a life after death integrated with the sea-mammal, the creature that had been looked upon as sacred. The seal was a creature that out-foxed many of its predators, with the sheer manoeuvrability of this mammal at speed in the water, its mastery of camouflage with spotted body and lozenge patterns, and its deception whilst on land and in the water portraying itself as having a head at either end of its body. With its ability to swivel its head around to face the opposite direction, the eyes of the creature, considered to be all-seeing and all-knowing, were constantly emphasised.

Many of the standing stones have the seal portrayed within an acute angle or a triangle, or as a diamond pattern with the head of the seal looking in two different directions at the same time, indicating the ability of the seal to swivel its head around through 180 degrees. This is similar to the two heads sculptured on the Bryn Celli Ddu decorated stone (Fig. 95).

The sarsen to the left (Fig. 112) has the head of a seal inscribed on the front face of the stone near the centre, with its snout and eye positioned as if looking upwards to the left. Once the reader has established this inscribed figure, look at it carefully once more and notice that the head can also look downwards to the right.

Figure 112 *Sarsen stones at Stonehenge.*

This feature of rock art was based on the lozenge design outline and is often included in the cultural artistic work of ancient people. It would appear that many people today have ignored the artistic designs found on rocks, and have discarded these symbols as a form of simplistic childlike art developed by early simple-minded humans having no relevant meaning or significance. How wrong people have been in not seriously attempting to understand and appreciate the meaning of the Stone Age art of circular spiral figures, inset and raised dimples, triangles, and lozenge designs. These symbols were not wholly abstract, but were in fact a record documenting a way of life for future generations to understand.

The people from the Wessex Culture had a very close link with the inhabitants of Argyll's Kilmartin Valley, who had their own large Timber Circle, only recently discovered in this ritual valley of the dead. The timber circle is some 153 ft. in diameter, and is located in an area high up on a terrace at the side of the valley, in line with the 'linear cemetery' of the Bronze Age cairns. It has been stated that the approach to the circle from the valley is reminiscent of the Avenue at Stonehenge. In this valley of the sacred dead are three outcrops of decorated rock, said to be the largest expanse of cup and ring carvings known in Britain.

Figure 113 *Symbolic symbols at Achnabreck.*

The boulder artwork at Achnabreck (Fig. 113) near Cairnbaan and the Crinan Canal, is described on a notice board, thus **"The design is relatively simple. Many hollows (or cup marks) surrounded by one or more rings. Additional lines or gutters radiate out from some of the cup marks. Notice that there is no representational art; no human figures and no animals."**

This is *not* the case, nor is it so simple; in fact it is quite complicated as the mammal of the seal can be observed, along with the lozenge design, stated to be gutters! This is a meaningful work of art expressing beliefs held for thousands of years. These ancient people had been recording their religious faith and life on these boulders, prevalent amongst the symbols being acute angles representing the beginning of a new life after death. Several of these patterns of the spiral of life are similar to the triple spiral design found at Newgrange, Ireland, representing the eyes and snout of the seal (Fig. 67) and to a single spiral of life shown on one of the stones at Temple Wood Stone Circle (Fig. 114).

The symbolic stone shown on this photograph is the side view of one of the stones forming part of the well-preserved Temple Wood Stone Circle. Towards the top of this stone is the eye of a seal, which is enclosed within a faint lozenge design; the pecked marks at the top are indicating the whiskers of the seal, which can be seen by turning the photograph clockwise. Lower down the stone, one can find the well-known spiral appearing as indicating one of the seal's side flippers.

Figure 114 *Temple Wood Seal Stone.*

Another interesting stone, shown in Figure115, can be found inside the Northern Cairn, forming part of the alignment of Cairns in the Bronze Age cemetery, at Kilmartin.

Figure115 *Inside Netherlargie 'North' Cairn.*

The North Cairn has a sliding door to enter the inner chamber, within which is an interesting cover-slab, decorated with axe-head carvings and cup marks. However there is a lot more to these decorations than has previously been discussed, such as the overall sculptured stone itself, which can be divided into two distinct designs. The first is the acute angle shown as if cut into the stone as a step, indicating 'A' for 'alpha', the beginning. Moving to the right within this acute angle one observes the eye and open mouth of a sea creature, indicating the emergence of the round head and eye of the seal, the beginning of a new spiritual life.

The second design is illustrating the head, eye and snout of a seal, again looking to the right. The cup mark indicating the eye is encircled by a further faint lozenge. The cup marks also indicate the camouflaged spotted pattern found around the body of the seal, and these same cup marks take the form of the eyes and mouth of the seal similar to the mammal's natural camouflage, including lozenge patterns and angles representing 'A'. Some of the stones forming the interior wall of this chamber have the head and eye of the seal shown within an angle.

In the recently opened Kilmartin House Trust Museum, Argyll's ancient past with its rich history has been brought to the attention of passing tourists. The Jet Necklace displayed at the museum is a replica of the Poltallach Necklace which dates back to around 1600BC. Jet was formed from the Monkey Puzzle Tree during the Jurassic period. The jet from which this necklace is made came from Whitby, Yorkshire, one of the few places in Britain where this material can be found. The lozenge design inscribed on this necklace (*see* Colour Plate 7) helps to confirm the religious significance and importance the ladies attached to wearing this necklace, and to their spiritual beliefs.

Recalling my holidays as a child staying with relations in a croft at Ardfern, in Argyllshire, we travelled over the hills and moors, spending time at Carnasserie Castle, visiting the standing stones and cairns in the Kilmartin Valley. Those were the days when there was time to catch a fine trout in Loch Awe, or sail around the sea lochs and islands accompanied by the cries of circling diving gulls, our progress observed by the bobbing heads of inquisitive seals singing like sirens on the rocks.

It was in Argyllshire in recent months that I came across yet another potential new megalithic site, where the ancient boulders are surrounded cheek to jowl with tree stumps recently felled. Movement is restricted by a great many large branches scattered all around, limiting access to this small but invaluable site, which is much smaller yet similar in a way to the triangular sculptured head of the Dwarfie Stane, Orkney.

In yet another area of Northern Britain, I came across an intriguing group of megalithic boulders, which may assist in a better understanding of the rare inscribed triple design symbols found on the Class I Sandside Symbol Stone (Fig. 116). This is the symbol also known as the triple vesica piscis as depicted on the Class II Halkirk Skinnet Stone, now in Thurso Museum, Caithness.

On one of these fascinating sculptured boulders are large multi-sculptured heads of seals (Colour Plate No.10). This boulder stands apart and, I believe, had been the frontal boulder of a series. To me it depicts the head of a seal with its mouth pursed. Viewed from different angles, other megalithic rock art symbols are also seen along with a series of smaller well-defined sculptured heads, as shown along the top right hand edge of this boulder (Colour Plate No.11). Another seal head appears on a separate stone shown at the very top right hand corner of the same photograph.

Figure 116 *Sandside Class I Stone.*

The remains of an oval type seal chamber is part of this group of boulders only yards away from the stone shown in Colour Plate No.11. The side entrance to this tomb is visible in the background of Colour Plate No.12, showing the large sculptured rounded head of a seal with its eye, snout, and mouth slightly open forming the shape of the front boulder. In the photographs of the entrance to this chamber, Colour Plates No.12 and 13, there is an inclined part of the stone positioned above the clump of heather as if attempting to get out of the chamber, again part of the ritual.

This is a large potential megalithic site, located by a flowing stream with many boulders depicting the seal. This area would appear to have been of significant ceremonial importance to ancient people. One very long tapered boulder representing the seal forms one side of a natural gully, where the water flows and cascades over further boulders and rocks set in its path. One boulder, shaped as a small orthostat or standing stone, had been placed upstream, while other stones were placed across the stream to create a weir. This to me had been part of the ancient people's ceremonial ritual of the seal attempting to reach up to a higher level, similar to the beliefs of the Japanese regarding the carp. The ground covering of boulders interspersed with peat and heather have megalithic rock art patterns carved upon them. There is a distinct possiblity of further burial cairns in this area. A grouping of large boulders observed from a distance gives the impression of a collapsed dolmen.

This appears to be part of a large ceremonial site, where the possible chamber, shown in Colour Plate No.12, is only a small indication of the potential for other significant finds in the area. The Royal Commission on the Ancient and Historical Monuments of Scotland were indeed very interested in the photographs of this discovery, and confirmed the only similar burial site known to them was the Dwarfie Stane, in Hoy, Orkney. The Dwarfie Stane is an isolated rectangular block of red sandstone roughly cut, with the chamber hewn through solid rock. It was instantly apparent to me when shown a sketch of this Dwarfie Stane that the triangular shape appearing at the front of the Orkney stone was that of the head of a seal. However I believe that this new burial complex is a more elaborate and interesting collection of Rock Art, confirmed verbally by the RCAHMS as 'quite a unique find for Scotland.'

Megalithic burial sites can even be traced out into the Atlantic to the tiny islands of St.Kilda. There on the Island of Hirta in 1997, George Gall, a geologist, and his wife, a botanist, from Cupar in Fife, formed part of a voluntary working party for the National Trust of Scotland. George came across a number of boulders with unusual carvings which could not be explained by archaeologists (Fig. 117). Opinions of well-informed individuals varied. These ranged from the markings being natural, to caused by differential rates of cooling of the various substances in the magna from which the boulder was formed, to reluctance to comment, although suggesting that it should be reported to the RCAHMS. This George intends to do, as both he and his wife are convinced that the markings have been made by early humans.

Being privileged to examine George's photographs, the symbols indicated to me the Rock Art of megalithic people who had inscribed these stones when paying homage to the seal in these remote islands. These symbols included positive artwork of inscribed lozenge designs along with the heads of seals, declaring a connection with burial chambers whilst recording the resting place of their dead. What I found quite fascinating was the similarity of this plan view of their sacred burial site to the aerial views taken of prehistoric sites throughout Britain.

Figure 117 *Hirta/St Kilda.*
By kind permission of G.Gall

Becoming more familiar in recognising and understanding many of these Rock Art symbols enables me to identify and locate megalithic sites, which may have gone unnoticed over the years or have been considered by many generations as features or flukes of nature. There are several sites in the Lake District, such as Helm Crag, towering well above Grasmere, possibly the best-known fell in the Lakeland. The shapes commonly referred to as 'the Lion and the Lamb' were sculptured by early man, but as seal heads! Yet again these early people were striving to reach the highest peaks to present their religious beliefs to the empyrean. They were obviously at home on these peaks and hilltops, and appear to have been peaceful people, not the savages described by the Romans.

I am now convinced that there had been a large population in this area, and that Mesolithic people physically worked upon many of the hills and mountains, with their unquestionable religious obsession to portray the prominence of the sacred seal to the skies above. The seal had been at the very heart of the Stone Age economy, an economy that had been universally known and respected by all in Western Europe. These people, whose beliefs can be traced right up to our present time, were highly successful in expressing their faith at sacred burial chambers.

When motoring over the Perthshire Hills to visit a replica of an Iron Age dwelling, built on stilts over Loch Tay, it was interesting on the journey to observe boulders with megalithic rock art symbols. Some were located at a fairly high position, again confirming the existence of early people dwelling in the higher reaches of our hills and mountains. Arriving at Loch Tay I visited the reconstructed crannog (Fig. 118) recently built opposite the picturesque village of Kenmore, Perthshire. The crannog with its conical thatched roof has been placed on the actual site of an earlier crannog built here during the Iron Age c.500BC. One interesting find was made by skin-divers who found a discarded wooden butter dish with butter still adhering to it after over 2500 years immersed in the chilly waters of Loch Tay. Obviously over the ages the ice-cold waters of the loch had preserved this unique sample giving us a better insight into how these people lived. Not far away is a man-made island, which would also have had a crannog built upon it, confirming that there had been a small community living on the shores of this loch, where salmon and trout still abound. At present over 18 sites have been located around this loch where crannogs were erected as a security against attack by wild animals.

Figure 118 *Loch Tay Crannog.*

Much later people also lived nearby hillforts for protection. One such hillfort looks over the scenic Loch Earn at St. Fillans, where the Hillfort of Dundurn had been built with oval ramparts based on the ceremonial vesica piscis. One can visualise the high priests sanctifying this hillfort and the people dwelling around it, indicating their continued belief in the culture of the sacred seal. The oval shape of the rampart may also signify the mouth of the seal as observed from an aerial view, with the hill as its head, and its eyes portrayed by a well or cairn. This is not fanciful thinking as there are hills which can take on this formation, such as the Ladle Hill, Kingsclere, Hampshire, an unfinished hillfort. Viewed from an aerial photograph, Ladle Hill can take on the profile of the head of a seal, round barrows in the area possibly indicating the eyes, and the earthworks representing the mouth. Professor Timothy Darvill, in his book *Prehistoric Britain from the Air*, pages 142–3, illustrates another aerial view of Cleeve Hill, Southam, Gloucestershire, which may advance my theories. At Dundurn Hillfort, where we find the ruins of a Pictish fortress, with the chair of St. Fillan built into the wall of the oval rampart, Glasgow University have carried out extensive research. Not all hillforts were originally built for defence purposes. Many of these structures were erected as part of the ceremonial and religious tribal centre.

Figure 119 *The Seal Overseer of Dundurn.*

Looking over to Dundurn Hill Fort is a megalithic boulder referred to locally as the 'Crocodile Rock', which over the years has been regularly daubed with paint to highlight the rock art features visualised by the artist. The painter had observed eyes and a mouth on this rock, but was unaware of the true animal shape sculptured to depict a seal, not a crocodile. This boulder, with its many sculptured seal heads, had been at the very heart of ancient people's religious ceremonial rituals in this scenic area of lochs and hills.

A local man from Crieff, knowledgeable on ley lines, has been able to trace an energy field passing under this stone and continuing across to weave in and around an oval shaped stone cashel, embracing the ancient church of St Fillan, lying between the ceremonial overseer seal rock and Dundurn Hillfort. The church may well have been built upon the site of a former stone circle.

It should be noted that in Perthshire there had been two saints bearing the name of Fillan, but at different periods.

Figure 120 Broch of Gurness.

Other large circular stone dwellings found in Northern Britain are called Brochs. One, shown in Figure 120, is the Broch of Gurness, Orkney. It would appear that the landowners of Orkney and Shetland had decided to build new circular dwellings sometime around 500–300BC. This was an important development from henges, earthhouses and wheelhouses. Brochs are unique to Scotland where over 500 had been built, many spread throughout Northern and Western Scotland and its islands. Shetland and Orkney have dense concentrations of brochs, as has the Northeast of Scotland. Single broch structures have been found as far south as Wigtownshire. Many of these imposing towers stood as single units but the Broch of Gurness also became the focus around which a settlement had gathered and expanded. With the development of new building ideas and skills the rectangular stone structure, outside the Broch of Gurness (Fig. 121), had been erected to impress, as it still does.

However the seal continued to be held in high regard, as can be witnessed around these islands. What has also drawn my attention to this rectangular building was a series of carved heads of seals inscribed on one of the building blocks located just above the number on Figure 121, at the beginning of the title for this photograph. This design is remarkably similar to the carved heads of seals (Fig. 47) showing the end design of the large bone comb found at Dunadd, Argyll.

Figure 121 *Broch of Gurness Settlement.*

Broch builders demonstrate that people of Britain were already designing and erecting complicated structures long before the arrival of the pagan Romans, many of whose villas were unable to withstand the rigours of our more severe climatic conditions.

An inscribed stone found at the Broch of Gurness is illustrated in Figure 122, showing early indigenous symbols referred to as being of Pictish origin. These symbols can be traced back to the Bronze Age ancestors of the Picts. The four symbols depicted on this small stone are as follows:

Ref.A Ref.B Ref.C Ref.D.

Figure 122 *Miniscule Gurness symbols.*

Ref.A: is a plan view of a rectangular burial chamber.

Ref.B: is described as a tuning fork! However at the top of this figure there are two concentric circles indicating a henge or stone circle as the

place of tribal origin. Note how they have retained the acute angle of 'A' for 'alpha', which is attesting the beginning of a new life, as it points to the chambered tomb, the last resting place prior to the regeneration of the spirit. 'A' also indicates the aperture as a symbol for the return of the dead to the womb of the seal, to a new spiritual beginning.

Ref.C: is illustrating a plan view of a rectangular burial chamber with a passage entrance located at either end of the burial complex.

Ref.D: is a rather faint rectangular passage grave, with the passage indicating the 'V' shaped tail of the seal. This design is rather similar to the standing stone found on the island of Gigha (Fig. 74).

Iron Age villages, such as the stone-walled Chysauster Village, Cornwall, did not at first glance appear to have differed greatly from the earlier houses built at Skara Brae, Orkney. During the late Iron Age people of the West Penwith area of Cornwall built courtyard style villages, used into the Roman period. The plan views of these settlements indicate the presence of a lozenge perimeter, witnessing a change away from the circular henge, although oval and circular designs can still be detected.

Figure 123 *Stretching seal.*

An upright seal stone can readily be seen as if it were stretching upwards to feed on the foliage growing from the top of the stone wall at the entrance to a dwelling (Fig. 123). Another seal head appears on the right hand side of this stone looking downwards. Several acute angles can also be seen on this stone. This is not an isolated case as there are many examples of stone seals to be found in this Iron Age village in Cornwall. The Cordon Ware pottery found at Chysauster is dated from the first century BC to the first century AD, some items still retaining the serrated triangular design relating to the beliefs of the people who continued to look upon the seal as an integral part of their way of life.

Rome invaded Western Europe, possibly to quell the developing religious beliefs of the people and to avenge the sacking of Rome by the Celts. The Roman armies conquered those who opposed them, suppressing the beliefs and culture of the people; they inaugurated their own lawcourts, introducing Latin and Greek. They were not prepared to consider or learn from the ancient people of Europe, whom they denigrated until they realised that the ancient cultures of Britain were converging and merging with the rise of Christianity from Galilee. For a military power such as Rome this would have been a strategically unacceptable position requiring decisions to be made to neutralise such a potential threat. By first invading Britain, and after several attempts to overpower England, they then attacked and sacked the city of Jerusalem, assuming they had contained the discontent, but failed to realise the depth of religious feeling and beliefs held by the people at the extreme ends of its empire.

People of Britain were looked upon as savages by the Roman army, who had methodically set out to suppress the culture of the Druids and their religion. Caesar had written about the people of Britain as being a race of people who were indigenous to these islands, stating that they were taller than the Celts. He referred to Britain as being at the heart of the Druidic tradition, whose teachings had spread all over Europe, from where scholars came to study the oral traditions and faith of the British Druidic culture. The Druids had a heritage of skills in mathematics in relation to numbers, astronomy, and to the pythagorean-like designs linked to the people of Gaul and to those in the Mediterranean area. The Romans acknowledged the Britons by having some British princes brought up at the Court of Augustus Caesar, which led to many noble families in England forming close ties with Rome. Later Agricola trained the sons of the chiefs of the Britons expressing a preference for their natural ability over the trained skills of the Gauls.

These historical facts belie the dogma of the Romans and their spurious rumours about the people of Britain being barbaric savages whom they intended to ruthlessly crush. Britain and Ireland had their own laws and democratic standards of conduct, a religious belief in life after death, and a society where women held a special place. Later in c.61AD this privileged position of women was violated by the pagan Romans, the rape of Queen Boadicea and her daughters causing the people to rage and rise in revolt against them.

CHAPTER 10
The Early Christian Church

*R*ectangular buildings, common on the continent, were also known and built throughout Britain at an early period. However, it was uncommon for a rectangular building to be built in order to promote a new faith, and a new way of life. Some early Christians had lived in circular beehive type constructions, from which developed rectangular oratory buildings with a gable end likened to an upturned heraldic shield, which can be traced to the triangular shape of the seal head. The gable end has a circular window, directly related to the seal's eye, and similar to the Gallarus oratory erected in the corbelled principle style at Co.Kerry, Ireland (Fig. 124). This central circle can also be witnessed on the symbolic heraldic design of the Iona Abbey Font (Fig. 125).

Figure 124 *Gallarus, Co.Kerry.*
By kind permission of the Office of Public Works, Ireland

The triangular design of the gable end with its circular window was instantly recognisable by the indigenous natives as the symbol of the head and eye of the sacred seal. The weather-worn outlines of seals have been sculptured on stones forming the apex of the roof at Gallarus. The gable ends of the Gallarus type pre-Romanesque churches were indeed symbolic, as the addition of a similar inverted design would reveal the figure of the vesica piscis, the bladder of the fish, the universal symbol known by the ancients which yet again refers to the seal. This is one of the designs portrayed at Stonehenge (Fig. 112) and also represented by the lozenge design at Newgrange (Fig. 68) and on the ceremonial seal stone looking over at Dundurn, St.Fillans, Perthshire (Fig. 119). Dividing this design in two may well be the origin of the architectural design of the European Gothic Arch.

This heraldic style of building had also been found in other areas of the country, and is similar in construction to corbelled beehive houses, along with other structures known as cleits. Cleits are found on the island of St Kilda where they were either circular or of the traditional oval design, with an entrance door located in the centre of the long oval sides, and were used later during the18th century for drying peat, birds and fish.

Figure 125 *Iona Abbey font.*

Pre-Roman Christian clerics were well aware of the significance of these heraldic designs, observed on the decoration of the font in the Abbey of Iona, the island on which St.Columba landed to promote Christianity among his beleaguered kinsmen. The Scotti had recently been soundly defeated by the Christian Picts, who had at an earlier date become Christians. In Figure 125 the circle of the eye of the seal is included within this triangular banner type emblem, this circle itself encircled by three fish. Appearing on this font are a circular henge and cross, surrounded by elongated sculptured sea-creatures indicating agility and swift movement, and recalling earlier pagan beliefs.

Figure 126 *St.Fillan's Crosier.*

The splendid ecclesiastical crosier and its case were carried as a mark of authority by another St.Fillan, also associated with Perthshire. The case on the right clearly shows the vesica piscis (inset) with the spirals of the tail of the seal at either end of the oval emblem. Above the oval is the cleric's head protruding from the 'V' opening of the gown. The lozenge design is observed on the staff to the left, whereas the case is of a more ornate interlacing pattern, relating to the seal and similar to the scroll symbols found on boulders, such as those at Achnabreck, Argyll (Fig. 113) and Le Dehus, Guernsey (Fig. 42).

Early missionaries understood the ancient beliefs of the people of Western Europe, establishing a close working relationship with the people. Both were developing along the same lines as those of the teachings of Christ, whereas the Roman Army was intent on imposing ruthless force by use of the sword to overthrow a culture which they recognised as a potential threat to the expansion and the glory of the Roman Empire.

Feeble excuses were made by the Romans for the butchery of ancient societies which they encountered. They quite correctly condemned human sacrifices made during religious pagan ceremonies, holding up their hands in sanctimonious horror and protestation that barbarous acts could occur in their Empire. Yet the Romans themselves worshipped false gods, while at the same time condemning the so-called barbarian tribes of the north, fearing that people in these countries would again rise up and usurp Rome, as did the Celts when in c.400BC they sacked Rome itself.

Yet, for every human sacrifice made by these ancient cultures, the Romans ruthlessly slaughtered thousands of people as they enlarged the Roman Empire. The early Roman Christian Church, where both Paul and Peter preached in Rome to the masses, was itself terrorised. Christians were persecuted and executed due to the political dogma of pagan Rome and its Emperors, who feared this new faith which people understood and were flocking to in their thousands, not only in Rome but throughout the Roman Empire.

The design of triangles with the circular eye of the seal was used by clerics to form a known and accepted symbol of a cross as shown on the standing stone located at Kilberry, Kintyre, Argyll (Fig. 127). The saltire design can be traced back to megalithic times, and later to the Chi-Rho symbol, which is also akin to the saltire lozenge design shown in the centre of the plan-view of the transept at Beauvais Cathedral (Fig. 128). This shows a link with architects using pythagorean principles in their design of the Cathedral.

Figure 127 Kilberry Stone.

Yet again early clerics were using megalithic symbols clearly under-stood by the indigenous people of Britain and France. The double disc in Figure 127 represents the henge, and the 'V' symbol indicates the 'A' for 'alpha', the beginning this time of our Christian faith.

This triangular shape of 'delta' is described today in a dictionary as 'the triangular shaped tract of alluvium at the head of a large river'. The an-cient people's translation of 'delta' would have included the triangular shape of the seal's head appearing on the surface of the water while it swam at the mouth or head of a river.

It is intriguing that in Wales the letters Ab, added in front of place names such as Aberdyfi, mean the head or the mouth of the Afon Dyfi (River Dovey). Early people were well aware that salmon entered the mouth or head of a river to swim further up to recreate their own species, in so doing creating a new life, and a new beginning; this may be one reason for having created the winding ceremonial avenues of the henges and linking them with the rivers. When Christianity arrived, it had also been adopted and looked upon as a new beginning, and the clerics became the Ab, the head of the Christian church, in many cases in a parish positioned at the head or delta of a river, while similarly an Abbot is the head of an Abbey. Christ to went to pray at the tops of mountains to Abba, Father.

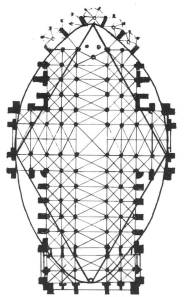

Figure 128 *Plan view.*

The head of the Church of Rome is of course the Pope, who is referred to as Papa. During the many ceremonial occasions the Pope, and his Cardinals and Bishops wear a mitre upon their heads. The mitre is an ancient pre-Christian symbol adopted by the early church and directly related to the vesica piscis, or 'vessel of the fish', which played a significant role in early Christian conversion. The symbolism of the vesica piscis can also be observed in sa-cred geometry, such as the pythagorean lozenged plan view of the Cathedral of Beauvais, France (Fig. 128), depicting the cross and the seal with flippers, similar to the aerial view of Belas Knap (Fig. 20).

The church is looked upon as a gateway linking heaven and earth. It is not unusual to find that many of our cathe-drals are based on the pythagorean geometry of this piscean and lozenge symbol. Portrait paintings have been made of Christ positioned within the surrounds of the oval or elliptical shape of the vesica symbol; some paintings have an elliptical border decorated with lozenge and circular shapes. The Greeks also borrowed and covertly used the vesica piscis symbol during the persecution of the Christians by the Romans.

The early pre-Roman Church in Britain, Ireland, and in Rome, even during Peter's and Paul's time and much later, still adhered to early people's ideas on evolution. [N.B. Both the bishop's mitre and the inverted cross on the mitre (Fig. 129) have several things in common with the symbolic standing stones, stretching upwards to reach the skies.]

Figure 129 *Scottish Episcopalian Vesica Piscis.*

The trapezoidal shape of the court tombs can be linked directly to the shape of the vesica piscis, said to depict the bishop's mitre, and illustrated on the notice boards of many of our churches in Scotland today. The emblem of the Church of Scotland is the burning bush depicted within the symbolic vesica.

The origin of the mitre can be traced back to the Stone Age. If one looks carefully at the side view of a bishop's mitre (Fig. 130) it appears as an open mouth delineating 'A' for 'alpha', the beginning, with the rounded protruding head of the cleric attesting to the rounded tail of the seal; from the tail of the seal another creature was to be born, creating a new beginning. To the ancient pagans the mitre portrayed a new beginning as a Christian. The sculptured birth of the seal had been carved on the Standing Stones to portray to early people the beginning of a new life after death, in the belief that man himself had originally evolved from a seal. On a person's death ancient people attempted to return the spirit of the individual to the origin of life as they saw it, to the ancestral spirit of a seal.

The Scottish Episcopal Church also embodies the vesica, complete with bishop's mitre and crosiers (Fig. 129). The two symbolic oval shapes on the mitre appear as the arms of the cross positioned on either side of the

central vertical coloured jewelled stem of the inverted cross. These two ovals or lozenge shapes also attest to the replica of the bulging eyes on the knuckle found on the tail flippers of a seal. On some mitres the replica bulging eyes of the seal had also been portrayed by the symbol of the cross, by embossed lozenge shapes or by jewels.

The two spirals at the top of the mitre are testifying to the chambered tomb of the dead, the final resting place and the symbolic 'beginning' of a new life after death. The triangular shapes of the various banners and shields are surmounted by the mitre indicating the banner as the head of the seal; the mitre then confirms the "seal" of authority of the church. The combined design of the banner and the mitre is an interesting emblem, as the banner can be directly connected to the gable end of the early church buildings (Fig. 124) and as shown depicted on the font design at Iona (Fig. 125). Both these designs can be traced to mesolithic man and to 'delta', the head of a seal. Now by adding the bishop's mitre, representing the tail of the seal, to the top of the banner, we have a very unique combination of the banner as the head of the seal and the mitre as its tail. This design may have been introduced from very early times, and can be related to the lozenge design within which are two seal heads shown at Stonehenge (Fig. 112) and observed on other megalithic tombs.

Figure 130 The bishop.

A side view of the mitre worn by a bishop is shown in Figure 130; note how the 'V' of the mitre appears as an aperture, representing the hind flippers and tail of the seal. There is, however, another fascinating feature witnessed by the ritual costume worn by the bishop; the white cassock, worn over the scarlet robes, highlights the red of the 'V' formation at the neck where the bishop's head appears as the 'beginning' of a new faith.

The dress of the bishop has been evolved from the ceremonial robes of the earlier ancient British high priests and can be directly related to the designs of the standing stones with their inscribed 'V' as depicted on our megalithic structures; recall the red ochre used by Neanderthals to cover the body of the deceased to begin a new life after death. Note how the Bishop's head protrudes from the 'V' to indicate in this instance the beginning of early Christianity.

Observe the triangular border pattern of the seal 'V'shaped head depicted clearly around the 'V' neck robe of Pope Clement IV (Fig. 131). Roger Bacon, an intellectual from Oxford, then living in Paris, had received criticism regarding his study of nature based on non-Christian thinking, such as the Arab and ancient Greek cultures. In turn Bacon sent the results of his studies, Opus Maius, to Pope Clement, clarifying his theories of mathematics, optics and physiology. With his manuscript went a plea to reform the study of nature throughout Christendom. Bacon wrote:

Figure 131 Pope Clement IV.

"For 20 years I have laboured specifically in pursuit of wisdom, abandoning the opinions of the vulgar."

Figure 132 Riskbuie Cross.

On the death of a pope, the body while lying in state is clad in scarlet robes and cap enabling the soul to be transferred to the beginning of a new life, as depicted by 'alpha'on his mitre and by the 'V' of the cassock indicating the beginning. This ceremonial dress of the bishop is remarkably similar to many of the standing stones. While many stones emerge to portray a head of a seal appearing from the top of a stone, Figure 132 portrays the head of a bishop appearing from a stone figure combining a cross and a seal.

The vesica piscis can be observed on the Riskbuie Cross from Colonsay (Fig. 132) sculptured in relief. This stone had formerly stood at the east end of the chapel of Riskbuie.

The figure depicted bears a strikingly close resemblance to a bishop in ceremonial dress. The head of a cleric is shown appearing from the 'V' mouth formation at the top of the stone.

This is similar to the Tlingit Indian (Fig. 60), a wooden carving from Northwest Canada, where the head appears from the open mouth of a fish. The seal stone cross with its two spirals portrays several meaningful and significant features:

1. A robed abbot with his hands emerging from within his sleeves as the spirals of life, showing the way to an everlasting life, as mentioned by Christ himself.

2. The spiral arms depicting the cross, but also referring to a seal's side flippers relating to the close affinity of the indigenous people with the seal and man's beginning, the symmetrical design of hind flippers and the Vesica Piscis pointing upwards to the new life in the firmament.

3. The spirals also representing the all-seeing eyes of the seal, while signifying the eyes of the Almighty watching over His people.

4. The stone recording the development of their religion with the coming of a new faith, and their acceptance of a new beginning as Christians.

5. The faint head of the seal as it looks downwards in its traditional manner on the bottom left hand corner of the stone.

Another example of the Vesica Piscis can be found in the ancient capital of Scottish Kings at Dunfermline in Fife. Above the entrance to Abbot House is a decorated panel of this emblem illustrating a seated Bishop, reading a passage from the Holy Bible to his flock, with his crosier in his left hand (Fig. 133).

Figure 133 Abbot House, Dunfermline.

In the National Museum of Moscow, a bronze coin can be seen with the design of the oval bisected by a spear.

Having spoken of the seal as a mammal, directly related to the vesica piscis, and the oval pattern, here is another example of an ancient "seal" of authority incorporated into the statutes of Balliol College, Oxford. I refer to the vesica piscis seal of Dervorguilla of Galloway. The Lady of Galloway confirmed the statutes of Balliol College, Oxford, at Buittle, near Castle Douglas, Galloway, Scotland, in 1282.

When John de Balliol died in 1269, Dervorguilla, his widow, took on the role of Patroness with enthusiasm and with the usual Scottish generosity. She continued to give her full-hearted support, and made the necessary arrangements on a permanent basis by the formulation of statutes (1282), and gave the Scholars a house, New Balliol Hall. The matrix of the first seal of the College, a further sign of corporate identity, was also engraved around this time.

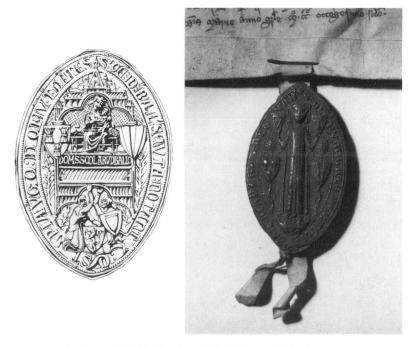

Figure 134 *Seals of Balliol College, Oxford.*
By kind permission of Balliol College, Oxford

Two of these oval or vesica piscis seals are illustrated in Figure 134, the 13th century College Seal and the Seal of Dervorguilla of Galloway. These Seals of Balliol College, Oxford, are of significant interest, not only to

Oxford, but can be related to the ancient people and to their megalithic oval and vesica piscis symbols. The similarity to ancient megalithic symbols is not confined to these elliptical seal patterns, as on the College Seal, 13th century, shown on the left, John de Balliol and Dervorguilla are shown supporting the College, with Virgin and Child; within this symbolic "seal" are many triangular gable ends of buildings, indicating the head of the seal; four triangular banners are also witness to the ancient tradition of the seal's head.

The Seal of Dervorguilla of Galloway is most important as this seal is portraying four coats of arms, possibly from the estates and properties she owned. But most intriguing of all is the manner in which the head scarf is positioned and placed around the head of Dervorguilla, the triangular shape indicating the symbol of power and authority.

Figure 135 *Emblem of the burning bush.*

Scotland's blue flag with its prominent white saltire is well-known as the flag of St. Andrew, Patron Saint of Scotland. This saltire also appears in the background of the emblem used by the Church of Scotland. This logo or seal is highlighting the burning bush, the eternal flame that will never be extinguished (Fig. 135). The design of the saltire can be traced back to mesolithic man.

The Church of Scotland is renowned throughout the world for sending out its missionaries to promote the Christian Faith, and assist developing countries with schools, hospitals and shelter for those in need of assistance. In many of our churches today, as shown in Figure 135, one can trace our ancient symbolism to the triangular shapes combined with the circle representing the head and eye of the sacred seal. Even the tall and not so tall spires of the church can be traced back to the ancient acute tapering body of the seal, as the spires stretch like the standing stones to reach ever closer to the skies.

Figure 136 *Church of Scotland, Crieff.*

One can relate the origin of Gothic arches to the gable end of the oratory on Gallarus (Fig. 124) and to the Vesica Piscis symbol. The simplified triangular shape forms the gable ends on this typical Church of Scotland building (Fig. 136) located in the town of Crieff, nestling in the foothills of the Grampian Mountains, an area known to the pagan Romans.

Seal of an early church with steeples

Let us attempt briefly to understand how our ancient religious beliefs amalgamated with those of the early Christians, especially when we consider that the present clerics in Rome, the Church of England and the Episcopal Church of Scotland are garbed similarly to the ancient cult ceremonial dress of the High Priests of our Pretannic ancestors. These holy men and women had resolute religious beliefs and faith going back to Cro-Magnon man and possibly even to the Neanderthals. This early religion also fostered belief in one God, in life after death, and survived for many, many thousands of years, without any of the mass-killing and brutality silently witnessed by some Christians, while Hitler's forces rampaged throughout Europe unleashing a reign of terror and mass murder on millions of innocents.

Our ancient faith in Western Europe had been evolving along similar lines to the preaching of Christ and His followers. One of those who had been particularly close to Christ, and indeed is said to have been one of his kinsmen, was Joseph of Arimathea. It is well known that Joseph was also a sea-trader, whose trading vessels were suitable for long sea journeys transporting ingots of tin from the mining ports of Cornwall. One of the traditional beliefs of metal workers in Cornwall is that Joseph of Arimathea was the rich man of the Gospels, making his money in the tin trade, sailing between the ports of Phoenicia and Cornwall. It is said that he brought Christ and His mother to St. Michael's Mount, in Cornwall. As the teachings of Christ and the language used were similar to those of the high priests and priestesses of Britain, it becomes more feasible that Jesus may have joined Joseph in his visits to Britain, and may even have begun His training in Britain before returning to Galilee.

It has been claimed by the people of south-west England, especially those associated with the tin industry in Cornwall, that Glastonbury was an area where Joseph preached to the Britons, and that one of his converts had been Gladys (Welsh for 'princess'), daughter of King Caradoc. Caradoc had opposed the Claudian invasion of AD43, waging war on the pagan Romans for nine years. During this time he demonstrated that as a charismatic leader he was able to enter another tribal area outwith his influence and unite the indigenous people to fight the common foe.

Eventually he was forced to retreat northwards and sought help and refuge from the Brigantes tribe who occupied Northern England. Queen Cartimandua, who led the Brigantes, betrayed him and he was taken prisoner, eventually being paraded through the streets of Rome in chains, prior to being taken to the Senate. At the Senate he gave a spirited speech which revealed him not as a savage but as an educated scholar and king, with his own government to support him. This contradicts the belief spread by the Romans that the Britons were a barbaric race. His rousing defence before the Senate not only enhanced his status in Rome, but has continued through the centuries to evoke a sense of pride among the hearts of the British people, ever since it had been recorded by Tacitus, the Roman historian, as follows:

" Had <u>my government</u> in Britain been directed solely with a view to the preservation of my hereditary domains, or the aggrandisement of my own family, I might long since have entered this city as an ally, not a prisoner. Nor would you have disdained for a friend a king descended from illustrious ancestors.

My present condition, stripped of its former majesty, is as adverse to myself as it is a cause of triumph to you...I was lord of oxen, horses, arms and wealth. Are you surprised if at your dictation I refused to resign them? does it follow that because the Romans aspire to universal dominion, every nation is to accept the vassalage they would impose?

I am in your power – betrayed not conquered! Had I, like others, yielded without resistance, where would have been the name of Caradoc? Where your glory? Oblivion would have buried both in the same tomb. Bid me live, and I shall survive for ever in history as an example of Roman clemency."

According to Tacitus, the whole Senate stood up and applauded loudly. Another Roman historian wrote:

"Rome trembled when she saw the Briton, though fast in chains."

The Emperor granted him a pardon and allowed him and his family to live in Rome, where they were given a large estate, known then as the Palatium Britannicum or British Palace. Caradoc and his family eventually became friends and allies of Claudius. The Damnonii tribe living in the south-west of England had probably paid allegiance to Caradoc, and another Damnonii tribe living in the Strathclyde area of Scotland may also have been governed by him.

This tribal contact between Scotland and Caradoc may well have been the reason for the Damnonii reluctantly accepting Agricola's advance into Scotland later in 81AD. Claudius changed Caradoc's name to Caratacus, and also the daughter's name from Gladys to Claudia. Claudia, born in 36AD, married Alus Pudens, a Roman senator and soldier. It is said that Pudens was stationed at Chichester during the Claudian campaign. In 1723AD an inscribed tablet was uncovered at Chichester recording a gift of land for the construction of a temple dedicated to Neptune and Minerva. This land may have been gifted by Pudens.

The changeover to Roman names made by the Emperor is interesting, as the name of an individual joining a clerical teaching establishment belonging to the Church of Rome is automatically changed; one example is Patrick Succoth (meaning 'home') which was changed to Palladius, which also stood for 'home'. St. Patrick's own name has never been recorded in the Church of Rome.

It was an ironic quirk of fate that in 52 AD Claudius had brought to Rome a senior member of the ruling British aristocracy especially as his family were Christians. Caratacus had a son, Linus, who it is said had been converted by Joseph of Arimathea, and had been taken as captive to Rome. He was freed with his family, and along with his sister Claudia, who married Pudens, took an active interest in the early Church of Rome. Pudens and Claudia are mentioned by St.Paul in his Second Letter to Timothy. One writer called Martial, a close friend of Pudens, in his Epigrams applauds her for her "illustrious birth", beauty, and great learning particularly in Greek and Latin literature, categorically mentioning her having been "born among the blue eyed Britons." It is worth noting that Claudia was referred to as a Briton and not as a Celt. Claudia along with her daughters and son had been looked upon as the 'lost disciples', prior to the arrival of Peter and Paul in Rome.

Based upon her own British culture which had been developing towards Christianity, Claudia with her husband and family set up an early Christian Church, today considered by Rome as a cult.

Here was the basic foundation of the Church of Rome being laid by the descendants of a British royal family whose home was a shelter and refuge for Peter and Paul. This had been confirmed in the 16th.century, by the Jesuit Father Robert Parsons who wrote of Claudia:

"Claudia was the first hostess or harbourer, both of St. Peter and St. Paul at the time of their coming to Rome."

It comes as no surprise that Claudia and her family, along with other ladies, had taken a leading hand in promoting Christianity in Rome. Ladies in Britain, especially those born to high rank, were at the forefront of religious beliefs and lawmaking. This was a tradition handed down as part of an ancient British matrilineal society.

On the site of Claudia and Pudens' house, the Church of St.Pudenziana, named after their daughter Pudenziana, now stands. They also had another daughter, Praxedes (Prassede), and a son, Linus, who was the immediate successor of St. Peter and ordained by Paul as the first bishop of Rome. Linus and all three ladies became Saints. St.Prassede like St.Pudenziana has a Church named after her. In the St. Zeno Chapel of St.Prassede's Church there is one of the finest Byzantine mosaics to be found in Rome. This mosaic work of art is referred to as "Theodora Episcopa" and, along with other murals, assists in confirming that women had aspired to become bishops in the early Church of Rome.

The Book of Saints published by A.& C. Black, London, 6th edition 1989, paperback edition first published in Britain in 1994 by Cassell, contains the full contemporary list drawn up by the R.C. monks of Saint Augustine's Abbey, Ramsgate, in which they refer to each member of Claudia and Pudens' family as follows:

"**Claudia (St.)** Widow. Aug 7.1st cent. A woman mentioned by St.Paul in his second letter to Timothy (4:21). A much later tradition asserts that she was a Briton, the wife of Alus Pudens, a senator, and the mother of SS.Praxedes and Pudenziana. This however is but a pious fiction." Page 127.

"**Pudens (St.)** Martyr. (May 19). 1st Cent? A Roman senator baptised by the apostles. In the past he was confused with a later (third century) Pudens who founded a church in his house known as the "domus Pudentiana"; from this the existence of a daughter, Pudentiana, was later inferred and spurious Acta created. He was by many identified with the Pudens mentioned by St.Paul (2 Tim 4:21)." Page 469.

"**Pudentiana (or Potentiana) (St.)** V. May 19. 2nd Cent. A legendary Roman maiden, daughter of the senator St. Pudens. She is said to have died at the age of sixteen. Her name does not occur in any ancient martyrology. Her cult was suppressed as unhistorical in 1969 and veneration of her is confined to her basilica in Rome." Page 469.

"**Praxedes (St.)** Virgin. July 21. 2nd. Cent. Said to have been the daughter of the Roman senator Pudens and sister of St. Pudentiana. One of the ancient churches in Rome perpetuates her memory. Since 1969 her cult has been confined to her basilica in Rome. Her church inspired a fine poem by Browning: 'A Bishop ordres his Tomb in St.Praxedes'." Page 465.

"**Linus (St.) Pope,** formerly Sept.23.d.c.79.The immediate successor of St.Peter in the see of Rome, which he ruled for **twelve years** (67–79). He was traditionally venerated as a martyr, but there is no evidence for his martrydom. His name is mentioned in the first eucharistic prayer. Cult suppressed in 1969." Page 346.

Why had Rome taken until 1969 to reach the decision to suppress the so-called cult of this entire family? It is very doubtful if Peter and Paul would have contemplated this drastic decision. It would appear that the historical evidence has been, in the Vatican's own words, "suppressed", even although Linus had ruled as Pope for twelve years, a lengthy time, and had been elevated to sainthood by the early Church of Rome. At the Church of Prassede the historical sarcophagus, containing the remains of both Prassede and Pudenziana entombed in ancient splendour, lies there

for all to see, yet the knowledgeable monks of St.Augustine's Abbey state that their mother Claudia was fictional! There are many murals in the Church of Prassede and Pudenziana which depict them both with Peter, Paul, Linus and other dignitaries. Obviously the Epigrams written by Pudens' poet friend, Martial, may not even have been considered, or had his writings also been suppressed?

If the Vatican has deemed it correct to suppress Linus, Claudia and family as cult figures, then what of the ceremonial robed gowns and dress worn by the Pope, his Cardinals and Bishops, relating directly to the cult of standing stones, stone circles and to the orthostats of the megalithic tombs of Western Europe? These customs were handed down from the early people as part of the same cult worship known to and supported by Claudia and her family who were already practising Christians. In Britain and Ireland this cult worship had been a prominent feature of the religious beliefs of ancient people who were progressing in their own way towards a new Christian faith.

Until recently it had been acknowledged that Paul had appointed Linus as the first Bishop of the infant Church of Rome, with his name recorded on a tablet on the walls of the Vatican, and in the Church of St.Paul-without-the- Walls built by Constantine the Great. This Church sprang from the site where St. Paul had been beheaded; medallions, found in the catacombs, were placed in the Vatican Museum recalling the close association between Paul and Linus.

In the second century, Irenaeus, the Bishop of Lyons in France, wrote:

"The apostles having founded and built up the Church of Rome, committed the ministry of its supervision to Linus. This is the Linus mentioned by Paul in his epistle to Timothy."

One paper written by a scholar after a recent visit to Rome sums up this amazing change of stance by the Church of Rome, as follows:

"Above all the Church of St.Pudenziana itself could not have been one of the major ancient Christian sites in Rome, which it undoubtedly has been and is, if it had been founded purely on a fiction which it has taken nineteen centuries to prove."

Both pagan Romans and the later Church of Rome have never attempted to understand the religions and beliefs of early people in Western Europe, or for that matter in any non-Christian country in the world. The growth of this early Church was actively encouraged by St.Peter and St.Paul, who along with Pudentiana and her sister, Praxedes, were later executed as Christian martyrs of the early Church of Rome. Sadly almost 1900 years later Claudia and her entire family are discredited by the very church they helped to found!!

It becomes clear that there had been at least two streams of thinking in the early Christian Church. Paul and Peter had obviously encouraged Claudia's European approach to integration with the early Christian Church, while at a later date Rome found it a prudent, political move to merge some of the European customs with the eastern practices, such as retaining the European High Priest's ceremonial 'V' necked overgown, scarlet undergown, mitre, and staff of authority, in an attempt to salvage some influence over her fast declining empire. To accomplish this they required to retain control of the new faith developing among the European countries' elite, the rulers and princes, as well as through the religious beliefs of the people.

In St.Prassede's Church there is a large circular porphyry with the inscription "Conditorium reliquiarum sanctorum martyrum in aedibus sanctae Praxidis", which indicates the well where St.Prassede hid the bones of the Christian martyrs. Here is evidence of St.Prassede gathering up the bones of martyrs, just as megalithic people had done in Britain during their ceremonial ritual of carrying the bones of the dead along the lined avenues that imaged river passageways to the ceremonial stone circles for the eventual transfer of the deceased spirit to the sky.

This memorial is confirmation of the development of a megalithic circular design that can be traced back to the stone circles, to the designs on funerary urns, and to the seal itself (Fig. 137). The circular disc of this concentric circle is encircled by a ring of triangles representing the heads of seals, a design which can be directly related to crescentic necklaces, such as the reconstructed Crescentic Arran Necklace (Fig. 86) and similar to the design of the crescent of the Logie Stone (Fig. 77). All the white triangle symbols are signs of purity pointing away from the centre, indicating the transcendence of the spirit from the skeletal remains to the hereafter. The double shallow denticulated ring is indicating the waves and water from which the seal had emerged and possibly returned to prior to the final spiritual journey to the heavens. On the death of an Egyptian Pharaoh part of his sacred travel in the underworld (purgatory) was conducted through water before being carried aloft by Horus, the falcon, hence a boat for this journey found in the foundations of a pyramid.

Figure 137 *Memorial to St.Prassede.*
By kind permission of Gordon Strachan

What is also fascinating is the Chi-Rho sign shown within the circular band which separates the triangles from the wave pattern. The origin of this saltire design is much older than at first imagined, and goes back to Neolithic man indicating the beginning of a new life after death, not a crucifix. The ring of acute angles indicated the heads of seals as if coming together at the resting place, in this instance the well in which the bones of the martyrs have been laid to rest, before beginning a spiritual journey to a new afterlife; the triangles also relate directly to the letter 'A' the 'beginning'.

The saltire configuration can be observed on the lozenge design shown on the chamber entrance of Newgrange, Ireland (Fig. 62) and is also symbolically witnessed there by the ring of recumbent seal stones. These recumbent stones form an unbroken ring, with the snouts of their stone heads as if touching to form the saltire 'X' in joint silent harmony and respect for the departed. This symbolism is part of the sacred ceremonial rituals attested by the raised Sarsen Stones constituting a close-knit circle at Stonehenge, and also explains the hexagonal shape of the Men-an-Tol Stone in Cornwall, where the acute angle formed is actually the saltire in reverse, again the triangular head of the seal.

The 'P' may have represented another emblem prior to the coming of Christianity, a symbol similar to the Key of Life, the Ankh, referring to the beginning of life after death. The Romans related the ancient megalithic saltire to the much later 5th century Greek 'X' for chi, and then coupled it with the Greek 'P' for rho, to form the first two letters of the word Christ, which to them suggested the beginning of a new life as a Christian. The cross on which Christ had been crucified had not been shaped as the saltire. Until now the saltire symbol had puzzled me. Now it can be shown that it is directly affiliated to the builders of the megalithic burial chambers with their lozenge shape designs, and also to the largest tombs known, the pyramids, the plan view of which seen from the skies forms a natural saltire, a further rather interesting connection with the Pharoahs of Egypt.

The cross, upon which Christ had been put to death by the pagan Romans, was repugnant to the people of Britain and Ireland. To the Europeans this was one of the cruellest and most barbaric of deaths that could be inflicted upon anyone.

The British Chi-Rho symbol had been included on the standards of Constantine's Roman army when around 406 AD he had led his men back to Rome via Gaul; it is said to have been used by the Christians in the fourth century, well over a century before the Greeks ever considered including the 'X' in their alphabet.

Another 'X' bisected by a straight line can be found inscribed on the smooth surface of a stone tablet, along with lozenge designs, at Skara Brae, Orkney, dating back to c.3000 BC. The early Christian missionaries were to develop and eventually claim and rebrand the chi-rho symbol.

Another example of the Chi-Rho symbol is shown on a lead baptismal tank (Fig. 138). Here three symbolic figures are cast on the Icklingham lead tank: the Chi-Rho symbol, flanked by 'omega' and 'alpha'. N.B. The saltire design has been formed by two individual 'V' symbols turned on their side, these special symbols coming together as if 'welcoming' the vertical staff of the High Priest. These symbols can be traced back to the early tomb builders, who incorporated the saltire design, and to the circling Newgrange recumbent stones (Fig. 94). The serrated border above and to the side of the symbols relates to water, and of course baptism by total immersion in water is a symbolic commitment made to God in acceptance of a new faith and a new beginning.

Figure 138 *Symbolic alpha.*

The acute angle to the left of the 'P' may have the small circular indentation indicating the eye of the seal. The 'P' symbol, referred to by the Romans as the Greek capital letter P, does not seem to tie up with the Mesolithic and Neolithic people who were sincerely religious, possibly having two tiers of democracy in Britain and Ireland, one relating to the priests and the other to the aristocracy, the land owners and chieftains who worked hand in hand with the religious clerics. This symbol could have been related to the crosier or staff, embodying the authority of the High Priest, who would naturally have presided over all ceremonies relating to burial rituals appertaining to their beliefs and customs.

One can now readily understand the development of the Western European burial chambers, as the early people ceremonially prepared and laid out their revered dead, in caves, cairns, and created massive portal burial chambers, long barrows succeeded by simplified wedge-shaped tombs, followed by round barrows and stone circles. They then awaited the rising of the sun at predetermined times of the year, using the shadows cast to pinpoint certain stone alignments in an effort to relate the rising sun with the rising of a departed soul to the sky. This type of custom can be traced to the islanders of St.Kilda, prior to their evacuation from the island.

There are at least three common factors to be found in these megalithic burial sites in relation to their ancient ceremonies.

– One was early people's religious attempts to transfer the dead to a new life after death.

– Second was their belief in returning the spirit of the dead to the ancestral spirit of the seal.

– Thirdly their belief in man's evolution from the seal was the common link to God, who had created the whale as the first sea-creature.

Humans did evolve from the sea, possibly as minute organisms that developed and grew over millions of years from a small stature to the upright form known today. Offspring today on average are marginally larger than their parents. When visiting museums, and observing the actual size of suits of armour worn by Knights of yore, the small stature of men never fails to surprise me.

From the Book of Kells is illustrated a solemn enthroned figure of St. John (Colour Plate14). The head of St.John is positioned centrally with the interesting symbolic circle located in the background. From the circle arises a circular band of banner shape triangles, complete with three dots relating to the eyes and snout of the seal. These triple dots are clearly observed on his clothing, four sets of these positioned within the triangular banner design pattern of his robes. Note also the book which is being held up for all to see has a large lozenge design on the front cover. The lower 'V' design shown as folds in his clothing are imaging the head of the seal. Observe the sandals worn by St.John, especially the one on his right foot, which is clearly portraying the seal with its frontal side flipper.

'Alpha', the beginning, 'Omega' the end, light and life are at the very root of our Christian faith which in turn had been founded on early man's beliefs. Christ himself was well aware of this fundamental fact. The word 'beginning' is referred to on many occasions in the New Testament, where in the Good News Bible, the Gospel of St.John, Chapter 1, v.1 to 9, reads:

In the beginning the Word already existed; the Word was with God, and the Word was God.

From the very beginning the Word was with God. Through him God made all things; not one thing in all creation was made without him.

The Word was the source of life; and this life brought light to humanity. The light shines in the darkness, and the darkness has never put it out.

God sent his messenger, a man named John, who came to tell people about the light, so that all should hear the message and believe. He himself was not the light; he came to tell about the light. This was the real light—the light that comes into the world and shines on everyone.

Book art was revived under King Alfred, with works such as the English modified version of the addition to a Psalter given to the monks of Winchester by Athelston. Figure 139 is my sketch taken of the original Athelston Psalter artwork produced during the 10th century, showing the continuity of the early art of symbolism and belief from Mesolithic times into the Christian era.

Figure 139 Athelston Psalter.

This work of art portrays the seated risen Christ shining against the background of darkness placed within the symbolic Vesica Piscis. The seated Christ is holding in His right hand the ancient Mesolithic inverted 'V' symbol of the beginning; behind Him in the background is the symbol of 'omega' located as if it were a moon or a star shrouded in darkness, but shining brightly indicating that darkness and death are not the end and relate to a new beginning. Christ's feet rest above the Church as if it were a footstool; note the triangular gable end of the building with its circular orifice, indicating the ancient head of the seal, an integral emblem of the early Church.

The Christian members of the Church are illustrated within the encircling design of a second pattern of the Vesica Piscis, where bishops with their 'V' robes and protruding tonsured heads gather on either side of Christ to bolster Him; the ladies are portrayed separately as upright pillars of the Church; the upper figures are a combination of clerics and male members of the congregation. All groups indicate their moral support for the central figure.

The Athelston theme portrays Christ risen from the tomb, having overcome death (omega), and portrayed in a new beginning as the true Light of the World. Light is a recurring theme in the New Testament, assisting us to realise the importance attached to early man's belief in light illuminating the darkness of a tomb. This is why ancient people paid attention to light from the rising sun as it cleared away the darkness, and aided the transfer of the soul of the departed to a new spiritual life.

The crucified figure of Christ on the cross, as depicted below on this ancient seal, illustrates that death was not the end, but the Beginning of Christianity. This is highlighted by three capital letters of 'A' positioned above the centrally seated figure of Christ. The banner on the lower section of the seal also illustrates the ancient symbol of the 'beginning'.

The beginning of a new life with its symbol similar to a 'V' or inverted 'A' was the most important part of ancient man's religious belief, and the foundation of Christianity, recorded in the Authorised King James version of the New Testament, in the Book of Revelation, Chapter 22, v. 13:

"I am the Alpha and the Omega, the first and the last, the beginning and the end."

Stone Age Alpha

Illustration Sources

The author wishes to thank the following for their kind permission to include photographs illustrated in this publication:

Figure No.
   6 .... Thorne, Roderick, Sanday, Orkney.
   8 .... Baxter, Colin, Speyside, Scotland.
 14 .... Thorne, Roderick, Sanday, Orkney.
 20 .... Cambridge University Collection of Air Photographs.
 41 .... Rankin, George, Chandlers Ford, Hants.
 42 .... Rankin, George, Chandlers Ford, Hants.
 43 .... Rankin, George, Chandlers Ford, Hants.
 53 .... Peterson, Graeme, Cheshire.
 61 .... O'Kelly, Claire, Cork, Ireland.
 62 .... O'Kelly, Claire, Cork, Ireland.
 66 .... Office of Public Works, Dublin, Ireland.
 67 .... Office of Public Works, Dublin, Ireland.
 68 .... O'Kelly, Claire, Cork, Ireland.
 73 .... Howden,W., The Gigha Hotel, Island of Gigha.
 77 .... Lines, Marianna, Collessie, Fife.
 90 .... National Museum of Scotland, Edinburgh.
 92 .... National Museum of Scotland, Edinburgh.
 95 .... Cadw Welsh Historic Monuments, Cardiff.
110 .... National Museum of Ireland, Dublin.
111 .... National Museum of Ireland, Dublin.
117 .... Gall, George, Cupar, Fife.
124 .... Office of Public Works, Dublin, Ireland.
134 .... Balliol College Oxford, Oxfordshire.
137 .... Strachan, Gordon, Edinburgh University, Edinburgh.

Colour Plates
No. 3 ...... Sentence, Peter, Cornwall.
No. 6. ..... English Heritage, London.
No. 7 ...... Kilmartin House Museum, Argyll.

       .... The Mermaid from Zennor. (Bottrell 1873, p288. Ian McNeil Cooke, 1993).
       .... Seal Mirror, Matthews, Caitlin, London.

Last, but not least, my thanks go to my wife, Sheana, for her understanding of my interest in my research and for editing this work, also for her encouragement and patience, while accompanying me as we set out to find the answer to our Mesolithic heritage.

Selected Bibliography

Ailred: *The Life of St. Ninian*, and Joceline: *The Life of St.Kentigern*.
Two Celtic Saints. Facsimile reprint 1989 by Llanerch Enterprises, Dyfad, 119pp.
Aldred, Cyril. (1988) *Egyptian Art*. Thames and Hudson, London, 252 pp.
Allen, J.R. & Anderson, J. (1953) *The Early Christian Monuments of Scotland*. Pinkfoot Press, Forfar, Vol. 1&2
Bahn, Paul G.(1998) *Journey Through The Ice Age*. Weidenfeld and Nicholson, London.240pp.
Butler, Rev.D. (1897) *The Ancient Church and Parish of Abernethy*. Wm. Blackwood & Sons, Edinburgh : London, 524pp.
Brooke, Daphne.(1994) *Wild Men and Holy Places*. Canongate Press, Edinburgh. 216pp
Cavendish, Richard. (1993) *Prehistoric England*. Artus Books, Orion Publishing Group, London,152 pp.
Carmichael, Alexander. (1992) *Carmina Gadelica Hymns & Incantations*. Floris Books, Edinburgh, 687pp.
Close-Brooks, Joanna. (1989) *Pictish Stones in Dunrobin Castle Museum*. The Sutherland Trust and Pilgrim Press Ltd. , 16pp.
Crawford, Barbara, E. (Edited by) (1993) *Scotland in Dark Age Europe*. St. Andrews, St.John's House Papers No. 5, (1994) St.Andrews, 97pp.
Cooke, Ian McNeil. (1996) *Journey to the Stones*. Cornwall Litho Redruth. 256pp.
Cunliffe, Barry. (1978) *Iron Age Communities in Britain*. Routledge & Kegan Paul, London, Boston, 460 pp.
Donaldson, Christopher. (1997) *The Canterbury Press Norwich*. 171pp.
Fleure, H.J. (1959) *A Natural History of Man in Britain*. Readers Union, Collins, London. 349pp.
Frend, William H.C. (1996) *The Archaeology of Early Christianity*. G. Chapman, A Cassell imprint. 412pp.
Gooch, Stan. (1989) *Cities of Dreams*. Rider & Co Ltd, London, 278pp.
Graham-Campbell, David. (1982) *Scotland's Story in Her Monuments*.
Grimal, Pierre. (1990) *The Dictionary of Classical Mythology*. Penguin Books Ltd. London. 466pp.
Gregory, Donald. (1989) *Wales Before 1066*. Gwasg Gwalch, Gwynedd, 144pp.
Hannah, Ian C. (1934) *The Story of Scotland in Stone*. Oliver and Boyd, London.
Harbison, Peter. (1988) *Pre-Christian Ireland*. Thames & Hudson Ltd, London, 208pp.
Harden, Donald. (1962) *The Phoenicians*. Western Printing Services Ltd. Bristol. 336pp.
Heald, Henrietta: Ed. (1992) *Chronicle of Britain and Ireland*. Chronicle Communications Ltd, England, 1296 pp.
Henderson, Isabel. (1967) *The Picts*. Thames Hudson, London, 228pp.
Hole, William. *Old Testament History*. Eyre & Spottiswoode (Bible Warehouse) Ltd, London, 147pp.
Hubert, Henri. (1934) *The History of Celtic People*. Bracken Books, London, 313pp.
Hunter, C. (1992) *Oban Prehistory*. Charles Hunter, Oban, 16pp.
Hunter, Rev.J., *et al*. (1896) *Chronicles of Strathearn*. David Philips, Crieff, 352 pp.

Jackson, Anthony. (1984) *The Symbol Stones of Scotland*. The Orkney Press, Kirkwall, Orkney, 254pp.

Laing, Lloyd & Jenny. (1993) *The Picts and the Scots*. Alan Sutton Publishing Ltd., Stroud, 172pp

Laing, Lloyd. (1974) *Orkney and Shetland*. David and Charles, London, 263pp.

Lines, Marianna. (1992) *Sacred Stones Sacred Places*. Saint Andrew Press, Edinburgh, 162pp.

Lynch, Michael. (1991) *Scotland a New History*. Century Ltd, London, 499 pp.

MacPhail, I.M.M. (1954) *A History Of Scotland*. Edward Arnold Publishers Ltd, 256pp.

Marsden, John.(1989) *The Illustrated Bede*. Floris Books. Edinburgh. 215pp.

Matthews, Caitlin. (1989) *The Elements of The Celtic Tradition*. Element, Dorset, 133pp.

McLellan, Robert.(1970) *The Isle of Arran*.Clark Doble & Brendon Ltd. Plymouth, 269pp.

McSween, Ann and Sharp, Mick. (1989) *Prehistoric Scotland*. B. T. Batsford Ltd. London, 192pp.

Meaden, Terence. *Stonehenge – The Secret of the Solstice*. (1997) WBC Book Manufacturers Ltd, Bridgend, Mid Glamorgan, Wales, 168pp.

Muir, Richard. (1985) *National Trust Guide to Dark Age & Medieval Britain, 400–1350*. George Philip, London, 256pp.

Muir, Richard. (1985) *Reading the Celtic Landscapes*. Michael Joseph Ltd, 288pp.

Nichol, Norman. (1979) *Life in Scotland*. A & C Black (Publishers) Ltd. London, 168pp.

Northern Archaeology. Neolithic Studies in No- Man's Land, Papers on the Neolithic of Northern England.Edited by Paul Frodsham.1996, *The Journal of the Northumberland Archaeological Group*. University of Newcastle upon Tyne. NE1 7RU. 201pp.

Philip, Alexander. (1925) *The Picts in Angus and Their Place Names*. D.H. Edwards, Brechin, 58pp.

Ravensdale, Jack. (1984) *National Trust Histories Cornwall*. Willow Books Collins, London, 95pp.

Reid, A.G. (1989) *The Annals of Auchterarder & Memorials of Strathearn*. Reprint by Perth & Kinross District Libaries, Perth. 353pp.

Renfrew, Colin. (1989) *Archaeology and Language*. Penguin Books, London, 346pp.

Renfrew, Colin. (1974) *British Prehistory*. Gerald Duckworth & C0. Ltd, London NW1, 348 pp.

Ritchie, Anna. (1989) *Picts*. HMSO Publications, Edinburgh: Glasgow, 64pp.

Ritchie, Anna and Graham. (1978) *The Ancient Monuments of Orkney*. HMSO Publications, Edinburgh: London, 72pp.

Ritchie, J.N.G. (1988) *Brochs of Scotland*. Shire Publications, Aylesbury, 56pp.

Roberts, J.M.(1996) *A History of Europe*. Helicon Publishing, Oxford. 628pp.

Roberts, J.M.(1996) *History of the World*. Helicon Publishing, Oxford. 952pp.

Robertson, Anne S. (1960) *The Antonine Wall*. Glasgow Archaeological Society, Glasgow, 98 pp.

Romilly, Allen, J. (1899) *Celtic Crosses of Wales*. J.M.F. Reprint 1989 by Bookbinding Services, Dyfed, 103pp.

Scott, Rev. A.B. (1917) *The Pictish Nation, Its People and Its Church*. T.N. Foulis,

Edinburgh : London, 566pp.

Simpson, W. Douglas. (1969) *The Ancient Stones of Scotland*. Robert Hale, London, 256pp.

Simpson, W. Douglas. (1925) *The Origins of Christianity in Aberdeenshire*. D. Wyllie & Son, Aberdeen, 37pp.

Spindler, Konrad. (1994) *The Man in the Ice*. Weidenfeld and Nicolson, London, 305pp.

Streit, Jakob. (1984) *Sun and Cross*. Floris Books, Edinburgh, 223pp.

Thomas, Charles (1986) *The Early Christian Archaeology of North Britain*. Oxford University Press, London, 253pp.

Trigger, B.G., Kemp, B.J., Conner, D.O. & Lloyd, A.B. (1983) *Ancient Egypt, a Social History*. Cambridge University Press, Cambridge, 450pp.

Wainwright, F.T. (1955) *The Problem of the Picts*. Nelson, 187pp.

Webster, Graham. (1986) *The British Celts and their Gods under Rome*. B.T. Batsford, London, 205pp.

Welfare, Humphrey. (1984) *National Trust Histories Wessex*. William Collins Ltd, Glasgow:London, 95pp.

Yoxon, Paul and Grace, M. (1987) *Prehistoric Skye*. West Highland Publishing Co, Ltd, Isle of Skye, 20pp.

Index

Index

Index

M

N

O

P

R

Index